"Thank God for this well-written and factual answer to the many deceptions and outright lies presented in *The Da Vinci Code.*

"After reading *Cracking Da Vinci's Code* you will realize it answers the many false myths used to purposely discredit Jesus Christ, the Bible, and basic Christian doctrine." AND THE CHURCH

—TIM LAHAYE
Co-author of the best-selling *Left Behind* series

CRACKING DA VINCI'S CODE

CRACKING DA VINCI'S CODE

JAMES L. GARLOW
PETER JONES

An Imprint of Cook Communications Ministries
COLORADO SPRINGS, COLORADO • PARIS, ONTARIO
KINGSWAY COMMUNICATIONS, LTD., EASTBOURNE, ENGLAND

Victor® is an imprint of
Cook Communications Ministries, Colorado Springs, CO 80918
Cook Communications, Paris, Ontario
Kingsway Communications, Eastbourne, England

CRACKING DA VINCI'S CODE
© 2004 by James L. Garlow and Peter Jones

First Printing, 2004
Printed in United States of America
5 6 7 8 9 10 Printing/Year 08 07 06 05 04

Interior graphics provided by Darcy Riner Graphics
Cover design: by Koechel Peterson & Associates, Inc.,
            Minneapolis, Minnesota
Cover art: *The Last Supper* by Leonardo da Vinci is Public Domain

ISBN: 0-78144-165-X

Dedicated to the Women in our lives

—our Mothers who gave us life … and love for God.
Thank you.

—our Wives who love us and affirm us.
We respect and love you. You are amazing.

—our Daughters who delight us.
You are so much fun to be with.

James L. Garlow

Peter Jones

In his book *The Da Vinci Code*, Dan Brown asserts that Leonardo da Vinci intentionally imbedded clues in his art that, when discovered and correctly interpreted, would reveal the truth about Jesus. While that is a convenient literary device, it has never been proven that da Vinci purposely included symbolism in his works for a future enlightened generation to unravel. Thus, the intention of this book is not to unravel da Vinci's code, for we are not convinced there ever was one. We refer at times to da Vinci's code, but for the most part we call it Brown's code, for we believe Mr. Brown is the original source of this code, not Leonardo.

DR. JIM GARLOW

Jim Garlow, an author, communicator, and historian, is heard daily on approximately 300 radio outlets nationwide in his one minute historical commentary called "The Garlow Perspective."

His academic journey included Drew University (Ph.D. in historical theology), Princeton Theological Seminary (Master of Theology), Asbury Theological Seminary (Master of Divinity).

Jim serves as the Senior Pastor of Skyline Wesleyan Church in San Diego, CA.

For more information, see www.jimgarlow.com

DR. PETER JONES

Peter Jones is director of *Christian Witness to a Pagan Planet,* an organization dedicated to equipping the Church in bringing the good news of the Gospel to an increasingly pagan world.

He is also Adjunct Professor of New Testament at Westminster Seminary in California. He holds a Master of Divinity from Gordon-Conwell Theological Seminary, a Master of Theology from Harvard Divinity School, and a Ph.D. from Princeton Theological Seminary.

Peter is married to Rebecca née Clowney. Together they are the parents of seven children. Peter grew up in Liverpool, England and was a close boyhood friend of John Lennon. He plays golf to a three handicap, and plays modern jazz piano.

For more information, see www.cwipp.org

CONTENTS

Acknowledgments

Special thanks to Gary Cass, Ross Chenault, Frank Kacer, Gerard Reed, James Smith III, and Alice Trotter for research assistance.

Enormous thanks go to Jeff Dunn, our editor and our friend. Without his enthusiasm, passion, and skills this book would never have come into being.

Blinding ignorance does mislead us.
O! Wretched mortals, open your eyes!

LEONARDO DA VINCI

"Let the prophet who has a dream tell his dream,
but let the one who has my word speak it faithfully.
For what has straw to do with grain?"
declares the LORD.
Jeremiah XXIII:XXVIII

CHAPTER 1

If everything we have learned about Jesus is false, what is the truth?

What is the underlying "code" in *The Da Vinci Code* — and why is it important that you know what it is?

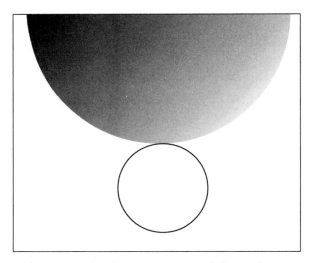

Before the code, the Divine Arc and the circle are
in their proper positions.

THE CODE THAT
SHOOK THE WORLD

*"What I mean," Teabing countered, "is that almost everything our fathers
taught us about Christ is false. As are the stories about the Holy Grail."*
Dan Brown, *The Da Vinci Code¹*

Everything you've ever learned about Jesus Christ is
false.

Is this possible?

Leigh Teabing is an expert in the ancient trail leading to
the Holy Grail. A former British Royal Historian, Teabing
moved to France to personally search through churches for
clues leading to the Grail. He is a multimillionaire descen-
dent of the First Duke of Lancaster and lives in a seventeenth-
century castle with two private lakes.

One more thing about Leigh Teabing: He does not exist.

Teabing is one of the fanciful characters in Dan Brown's
runaway best-seller, *The Da Vinci Code*. A fun, fast-paced sus-
pense novel, *The Da Vinci Code* debuted at number one on the
New York Times best-seller list, quickly hit the number-one
position with every major best-seller list in the United States,
and has been translated into more than forty languages. A
year after its publication, *The Da Vinci Code* has sold more than
six million hardback copies. Clearly, the fictional Leigh

Teabing—as well as Brown's main character, Robert Langdon—has a strong platform from which to share his convictions about Jesus Christ.

But Dan Brown is very real. And the ideas he presents about Christianity, spoken through Langdon, Teabing, and other characters in his book, are causing many to question what they have always believed to be true about Jesus.

It is time to separate fact from fiction.

The Da Vinci Code starts out with a ghastly murder in the Louvre Museum in Paris. The police call in Robert Langdon, a professor of religious symbology at Harvard, to help unravel the mysterious clues left near the corpse. On and around the body are riddles, which—when solved by Langdon and police cryptographer Sophie Neveu—lead to clues hidden in plain sight in the art of Leonardo da Vinci.

Did Mary Magdalene and Jesus marry and have a child?

Langdon learns that the murdered curator of the Louvre, Jacques Saunière, was not only the estranged grandfather of Neveu, he was also the Grand Master of an ancient society entrusted with guarding a secret that, if revealed, would threaten the very existence of the Christian church. Saunière died protecting the location of the proof of the Holy Grail.

Racing through the streets of Paris, to Teabing's exotic estate, to London aboard an unregistered flight, Langdon and Neveu try to stay one step ahead of the French police, an albino killer, and a mysterious man who is orchestrating this deadly search for the Grail. Intricate symbols and riddles lead Langdon and Neveu to the exciting conclusion, where the location of the Grail is revealed.

THE BIG COVER-UP

Throughout the novel, Robert Langdon teaches Sophie Neveu about the code—how to find the "true" Holy Grail. We find out that the Grail is not what we thought it was. The Grail, according to Langdon, is such a great secret that, if it were exposed, Christianity as we know it today would cease to exist. But it is not an *object* that author Dan Brown, through his protagonist Langdon, wants to reveal to us. And it is not just the secret location of this religious icon that so many have died to protect. The very substance of the Grail itself is at the core of this mystery. In the past, we have been led to believe that the Holy Grail—if it ever existed—is the cup Christ drank from at His last supper, and then was used by Joseph of Arimathea to collect blood from the crucified Christ. But according to Dan Brown's characters—Langdon and Teabing—the true Grail is not a thing, it is a person.

The Holy Grail is Mary Magdalene ... the mother of the royal bloodline of Jesus Christ (253).

Brown asserts that Mary Magdalene and Jesus were sexual partners and had a child together. When Jesus died, Mary fled from the other disciples, who were jealous of her relationship with Jesus, and lived in a Jewish community in France with their child. There is documented proof of this assertion, according to Brown, proof that has been guarded since the days of the Crusades by a secret organization known as the Priory of Sion. Hints of this secret can be found hidden in paintings and drawings by da Vinci and other artists throughout history, if only one knows how and where to look.

These theories are not new. As a matter of fact, Brown freely references other books in *The Da Vinci Code*, books that explore this theory of Mary Magdalene and Jesus. Most prominent among these other works is *Holy Blood, Holy Grail*, a 1982 release by Michael Baigent, Richard Leigh, and Henry Lincoln. (Brown's fictional character Leigh Teabing is an anagram of Baigent and Leigh.) The hypothesis that Jesus produced a child, or children, with Mary has been around for centuries. So why do we feel it necessary now to respond to it? Why did we set out to crack da Vinci's "code"?

JESUS: LOVER AND FATHER?

Many of the millions who have read *The Da Vinci Code* have enjoyed it solely as an entertaining mystery story. The action is tight—cliff-hangers at the end of just about every chapter propel the reader forward. Watching Langdon and Neveu solve each new riddle makes for a book that is hard to put down. And Brown uses a standard formula in romance writing: over-the-top characters against an exotic, but flat, background to create a story that appeals to both men and women, evidenced by the number of both sexes who have bought and read the book so far. Many of these readers have already moved on to the next book in their "to-be-read" pile.

Yet there are many readers of Brown's book who are now confused about just who Jesus really is. These readers are turning away from what they thought to be true to grasp a mangled mass of bizarre claims cleverly portrayed as a work of history in a work of fiction.

Cracking Da Vinci's Code is for you if you have stopped to ponder Brown's "code" woven into his novel. It is for you if you are now questioning all you have learned about Jesus. We are writing for you if you are now saying, "I once thought of Jesus as the Son of God, but I guess I was wrong. He is simply a man after all." For your sake, and His, we feel we must respond.

Many readers of The Da Vinci Code are now confused about who Jesus really is.

David Klinghoffer, writing in the *National Review*, sees the great danger in Brown's story:

> What's at stake in *The Da Vinci Code* is nothing less than traditional Christianity itself ... The founder of Christianity had a daughter, Sarah, by Mary Magdalene. If true, this theory would overturn some of the central beliefs of Christians.[2]

If true. Two very important words to consider. If Dan Brown is simply making up a plotline and including far-fetched fantasy, then this response would not be necessary. But Brown maintains that all he is writing is real. While being interviewed on NBC's *Today Show*, Brown defended the material he used in the book:

> MATT LAUER: How much of this is based on reality in terms of things that actually occurred?
>
> DAN BROWN: Absolutely all of it. Obviously, Robert Langdon is fictional, but all of the art, architecture, secret rituals, secret societies—all of that is historical fact.[3]

There is a reason Brown wants to stress his work is factual. ┼He wants you to come away with a new mindset.

"One of the aspects that I try very hard to incorporate in my books is that of learning," said Brown in an interview with *Bookpage* magazine. "When you finish the book, like it or not, you've learned a ton."[4] So Brown the novelist is also a teacher. And, like many good teachers, he begins his lesson by calling into question what you always thought was unquestionable.

- Jesus had sexual relations with Mary Magdalene?
- Our Bible is the construct of Constantine's political whims?
- The church has it in for women?
- Jesus was "voted" divine at the Council of Nicaea?

We can't honestly embrace these ideas, can we? After all, we have historical facts to show each of these claims to be false. Brown, however, has his own ideas about history and how much it can be trusted:

"It's interesting to note," says Brown, "that since the beginning of recorded time, history has been written by the 'winners' (those societies and belief systems that conquered and survived).

"Many historians now believe (as do I) that in gauging the historical accuracy of a given concept, we should first ask ourselves a far deeper question: How historically accurate is history itself?"[5]

HISTORY OR HOAX?

With that single question, Brown tosses out all traditional historical fact, everything we have built on through the centuries. *How accurate is history?* This is a pivotal recurring question in our postmodern society. It is also an echo of Pilate's question when faced with an innocent man he was condemning to death: "What is truth?" (John 18:38). By tossing aside the notion that there is such a thing as objective truth, we have nothing solid to hold on to. Thus we find ourselves adrift in a sea of confusion and doubt. To the contemporary audience, any method of recording or rewriting history is just fine. Brown discounts much of accepted history because it was written by the church. And winners write history. Yet, he

Brown asserts that everything he presents in The Da Vinci Code *is "historical fact."*

25

says everything he presents in *The Da Vinci Code* is "historical fact." So who are the new "winners" that Brown relies on for his historical facts?

These winners are obviously those who agree with his version of Jesus, Mary Magdalene, and the teachings of the Bible. He couches these beliefs in symbols, hidden messages in paintings, and ancient documents that were not even accepted as viable at the time of their writing. Many of these so-called "facts" on which Brown hangs his theories are easily discounted as false. While our main goal with this book is not to point out all of the errors Brown makes in *The Da Vinci Code*—and they are numerous—we will look at some interesting facts in sidebars throughout the chapters.

What does the "code" have to do with you and your beliefs?

Our main purpose in these pages is twofold. First, we want to reveal the real "code" that Brown has weaved throughout his story. What is this code? How can you recognize it in today's world? What does this code have to do with you and your beliefs? We will show you that Brown's code is far more dangerous to your soul than the fictional da Vinci code.

Second, we want to respond to the Holy Grail story. Perhaps it will surprise you to learn that we, Jim Garlow and Peter Jones, believe in the "Holy Grail." And it may further shock you to hear us say that Dan Brown almost has it right. We are going to reveal to you not only *what* the Grail is, but *where it is today.*

To help us along our path, we will introduce you to the fictional Carrie Williams. Carrie has many questions about life and her place in it, just as you no doubt do. Maybe you will see yourself in Carrie, or perhaps in one of the other people we will meet. Carrie's questions are meant to help you focus your own questions regarding the code we will be exploring.

Finally, as we begin this venture together, we're suggesting some additional resources that may prove helpful in cracking Brown's code. If you have a copy of *The Da Vinci Code*, keep it nearby. Also, find a copy of the Bible. It does not matter what version you have—we will draw from various well-known translations; whatever you feel comfortable with is great. At the end of our presentation, the publisher has provided a readers' guide to help you process the issues in this book—on your own, or preferably, as part of a discussion group.

The web sites listed below contain even more information that would not fit on these pages. Feel free to browse the sites to get a fuller explanation of any topic we cover.

Now, let's get started cracking da Vinci's code.

www.jimgarlow.com
www.cwipp.org
www.breakingthedavincicode.com

27

CHAPTER 2

Is it true that the sexual union between man and woman is the only way to "achieve *gnosis*—the knowledge of the divine" (308)?

Is it true that the church through the ages "recast" sex between man and woman as a "shameful act" (125)?

Is it true that the church has repositioned sex as evil in order to combat a threat to its base of power (239)?

"The Code"—even the portion pertaining to sex—if left unchallenged, systematically deletes a portion of the Divine Arc.

GOD'S SECOND BEST IDEA

Holy men ... now feared natural sexual urges
as the work of the devil (125).

"Let's head up to my room, Carrie. My roomie's only going to be gone for another hour."

"But it's so nice out here, Daniel. Why can't we just walk or sit in the sun for a while?"

"Because," he said in a loud whisper, "we can't do what I have in mind out here."

"I don't think I'm ready for that right now, Daniel."

Daniel's hand slipped down onto Carrie's hip as he pulled her closer to him. "Come on. I thought you Women's Studies people were into sexual freedom. Just think of it as extra credit for one of your classes."

Carrie didn't even try to keep her temper. Wheeling out of Daniel's grip, she turned on him and looked straight up into his eyes. "Listen, and listen good. If we Women's Studies 'people' have learned anything, it's that we don't have to be 'boy toys.' I was not put on this earth for your enjoyment. My body is my own, and I will not have you using it."

"Look, Carrie," said Daniel, not even trying to keep his voice down, "I didn't say you were my toy. And I do respect you. It's just that I thought we shared the same feelings for each other. And most people I know who share these feelings enjoy expressing them in a certain way."

Carrie walked along in silence for a while, then saw an open bench. She sat down and left room for Daniel to join her, but he remained standing. "Daniel, I don't expect you to understand this, but I'm looking for something more than just ... physical fulfillment. I'm looking for someone to fill my heart—I guess you could call it my soul. And just having sex, well, in my experience, it doesn't seem to do it."

Daniel sighed and sat down next to Carrie. He stretched out his legs and put his arm around her shoulders. "It's interesting you put it that way," he said, smiling. "Just last week we had a visiting professor from Cornell talk about sex in a way I never thought of before. This guy said we should think of sex as mystical and spiritual. He said guys can experience a level of divinity only when united with a woman. Something about the 'sacred feminine.'"

Carrie looked up at Daniel, excited to hear what he had just said. This was what she was looking for—experiencing a level of divinity. But one look at Daniel let her know that these were just words to him.

"So, what do you say? You want to experience the divine?" His smirk made him look less like a twenty-one-year-old college senior and more like a sixteen-year-old adolescent. Carrie knew it was time to move on.

"Daniel, it's been fun talking with you these past few weeks. But I don't think we're right for each other. I think we need to—"

Her last words were lost as Daniel jumped up and strode down the sidewalk. He shouted back over his shoulder, "I'm dumping you! You hear me? I am the one who dumped *you!*"

Carrie suddenly felt cold. She got up and wearily made her way back to her dorm.

Carrie's roommate for this semester, Jen, was seldom in the room at the same time as Carrie, so they hadn't really bonded. Carrie was surprised to find Jen at her desk when she returned. Jen was eating a salad from a takeout container.

"Hey, Carrie. Thought you'd be out enjoying the weather." She shoveled food into her mouth at a pace that belied her petite frame.

"No," Carrie sighed. "I just broke up—if you want to call it that—with Daniel. Turns out he was just about sex."

"Hmph," said Jen with a mouthful of food. "What's new? What guy isn't just about sex?"

There was something about Jen that made Carrie feel comfortable. She popped open a Diet Coke and sat down. "When was the last time you had a boyfriend, Jen?"

Jen swallowed a forkful of salad before answering. "Never. I don't like boys." Carrie laughed. She hadn't heard the phrase "I don't like boys" since grade school back in Connecticut. Carrie asked Jen if she had ever been dumped by a guy. "Nope, never," Jen answered. "I have never had a boyfriend, and I never will. I learned at an early age that I was wired a different way. I find the fairer sex to be, um, fairer. Not that all of my relationships with girls have been perfect. Tamra and I, uh, we broke up on Valentine's Day. She left, I stayed. I think I'll take a break before I get involved with someone again."

Carrie should not have been shocked. After all, as part of her Women's Studies curriculum she had taken Lesbianism: a Cultural Awakening. She had had many conversations with those in her classes who declared their sexual orientation to be homosexual. She accepted them, but she had no idea that her roommate of nearly three months was a lesbian.

"You didn't know I was gay, did you?" Jen asked. "Have you ever considered that you don't really need a male in your life? You carry in yourself all that you need to be complete."

"What do you mean?" asked Carrie.

"The sacred feminine. The perfect circle. Completion. Wholeness."

Carrie sat back as she heard the phrase for the second time that day.

"Look," continued Jen, "I have a book that explains it much better than I can. And it's a fun read. It's called *The Da Vinci Code*. It's a novel, but it's not all fiction. There's a lot of truth in it. As a matter of fact, I'm part of a readers' group that's discussing it. You can come with me if you want."

Carrie hadn't read a book other than her assigned texts in nearly four years. Spending time with a novel sounded like a good idea. *Better,* she thought, *than fighting off advances from guys like Daniel.*

"Count me in," said Carrie. "But first, tell me more about the sacred feminine."

———※◆◆———

The *Da Vinci Code* is not a sex book. And yet it is a book very much about sex.

As we progress through the novel, we find more references to sexual repression in the church. We read about sexual rituals that allow one to truly know God. And we see the church through the eyes of non-believers: a church that is so power-hungry it suppresses a natural, pleasurable act given by God to be fully enjoyed by humans.

Is it true that the sexual union between man and woman is

the only way to "achieve *gnosis*—knowledge of the divine" (308)?

Is it true that the church through the ages "recast" sex between man and woman as a "shameful act" (125)?

Is it true that the church has repositioned sex as evil in order to combat a threat to its base of power (309)?

The Da Vinci Code is ultimately—when pressed to its not-so-logical conclusion—an appeal for free sex, separate from the parameters established by God. This is one factor that will make *The Da Vinci Code* quite popular: giving people the approval to fulfill their desires with no commitment, no strings attached. Unfortunately, this kind of "freedom" comes at a very high cost in today's world.

Brown's *Hieros Gamos* is no sacred union. It is simply free sex disguised by using Neo-Pagan quasi-religious language. A prime example of this fact is seen when Robert Langdon tells of lecturing a group of students at Harvard about finding "divinity" during times of sex. The college

✠ THE LOUVRE MUSEUM

The Louvre in Paris, France was opened in 1793 as a way for the common person to experience the great art throughout history. Paintings and sculptures dating back to the sixth century B.C. are among the exhibits.

The museum is housed in a palace that dates back to the thirteenth century. In front of the main entrance stands the I.M. Pei-designed glass pyramid, made up of 675 pieces of glass.

The three most viewed works of art in the Louvre are the *Venus de Milo* and *Winged Victory* statues, and da Vinci's painting, *Mona Lisa*. Many tourists rush through the other 300,000 works of art just to see these three.

The *Mona Lisa* is the most visited painting in the world, with more than five million people annually coming from around the world to see it. The painting is displayed behind a pane of bulletproof glass.

The Hieros

Gamos *of*

paganism is no

sacred union.

women purportedly understood Langdon's "religious" explanation. In a not-so-subtle statement of male-bashing, the men in the classroom giggled immaturely. After all, Langdon notes, they were still boys.

In reality, Brown, through his character Langdon, is using a philosophical device called _casuistry_. Casuistry is using well-thought-out and well-presented reasoning, especially on moral issues, in order to justify what the individual wants to do. The male students, however, were not as ignorant or immature as Brown portrayed them. They saw through the charade of sophisticated ritual and logic. They knew exactly why they wanted their dates in bed! Langdon had just given them one more line to use on unsuspecting dates, and with a religious rationale to boot.

SEX: WHAT WAS GOD THINKING?

Sex is universal. All of us are sexual beings. The first description for every one of us (whether at birth or earlier by sonogram) is sexual: "It's a boy" or "It's a girl." We will not be referred to as an "it" ever again. We will be a "he" or a "she," each referring to a specific sexual context: male or female.

Whether male or female, we all share one thing in common: We came into existence through sexual intercourse. It took a man and a woman coming together in a passionate act to give us life. Sexual union is the way we, as well as many other species of animal, were made to reproduce.

Sexual activity is not an option if the human race is to continue to exist. But was sex created only for procreation? Did God have something more planned for us when He created us with sexual desires?

The answer is a resounding yes! God had much more in mind for us when He made our bodies and emotions. Sexual union and pleasure is a God-endowed part of our physical, emotional, and spiritual blueprints. But, like so many things God created for our enjoyment, we have corrupted and warped His plans. Instead of abundant pleasure and joy, our ways result in pain, disappointment, and—ultimately—separation from God.

Agape vs. Eros

I (Jim) wrote my master's thesis on the Greek word *agape*, contrasting it with *eros*. *The Da Vinci Code* profoundly cheapens true love when it states that the "Rose ... is also an anagram of Eros, the Greek god of sexual love" (254). According to Brown, "The Rose has always been the premiere symbol of female sexuality ... [T]he blossoming flower resembles the female genitalia, the sublime blossom from which all mankind enters the world" (255). (A correction is needed. *All* mankind did not enter the world that way. Adam and Eve were created by God. This is not a slip on Brown's part. It is significant in that it denies the role of the Creator, a major part of understanding the "code.")

No honest woman wants to be loved only erotically, as in *eros*—only for her looks. Otherwise, she will always feel vulnerable to the next better-looking woman who catches her lover's eye. *Eros* loves only for what it can get out of the other person. When there is no more to get, the *eros* love is gone. No sane human being wants to be treated that way.

C. S. Lewis writes in *The Four Loves* about this type of selfish, sexually driven emotion:

> The thing is a sensory pleasure; that is, an event occurring within one's own body. We use a most unfortunate idiom when we say, of a lustful man prowling the streets, that he "wants a woman." Strictly speaking, a woman is just what he does not want. He wants a pleasure for which a woman happens to be the necessary piece of apparatus. How much he cares about the woman as such may be gauged by his attitude to her five minutes after the fruition (one does not keep the carton after one has smoked the cigarettes).[1]

What woman would want to be loved only in the way of *eros*? What woman wants to be the empty cigarette carton, waiting to be disposed of? Yet, that essentially is the form of love Brown holds up as the highest form in *The Da Vinci Code*. This is classic paganism. With no connection between the Creator and the created, there is no reason to value individuals. Follow Dan Brown's thesis, and women will at best mutually participate in fulfilling *eros*-driven lust. Now *that's* at least anti-spiritual, if not anti-feminine. It reduces sexuality to the merely physical.

Deep within every woman—in fact, every person—there is a longing to be loved with *agape* love: that is, loved because we have value; loved because we are created by God. God loves us with this *agape* love, and we are to love each other the same way. The Bible, the church, and Christian tradition, with their insistence on loving others with *agape* love, value people, who are treated with dignity and respect.

Is the Bible Anti-Sex?

It would seem, at least from Brown's point of view, that the Bible and the church are both anti-sex. When Langdon informs the impressionable Sophie that the church is against sex, is he historically correct? Before looking at the church's view, let's see what the Bible has to say on the subject of sex.

We have two books: One is an engaging novel by Dan Brown; the other is the Bible. Both talk about sex. It is not the central message of either—yet it plays a significant role in both. The Bible has numerous key concepts regarding sex and sexual expression. And this Bible, being the source of all truth for the church, is full of beautiful references to sexual pleasure between man and woman. As a matter of fact, the Bible is an advocate of *maximum sexual pleasure*. In Genesis 26:8 (NLT), Isaac is seen "fondling" his wife. Proverbs 5:18–19 encourages some rather explicit sexual enjoyment between husband and wife. And the Song of Songs (Song of Solomon) in the Old Testament is nothing less than an erotic love poem filled with all sorts of sexual expression.

In the New Testament, the references to sexual activity are not as poetically written. Nevertheless, in 1 Corinthians 7:1–6, Paul tells husbands and wives that they no longer own their own bodies; rather, the husband's body belongs to his wife, and the wife's to her husband. In other words, they are *agape*

Sex orgy

As a matter of fact, the Bible advocates maximum sexual pleasure.

to seek mutual satisfaction in their love-making. Furthermore, the marriage bed is treasured and honored as pure (see Hebrews 13:4). Sexual activities and pleasure are normal, expected, and encouraged within a marriage.

The Bible gives the church and individual believers principles for every aspect of life. Yet Brown ignores the positive teachings the Bible offers on sexual expression, substituting instead a ritual sex orgy (the *Hieros Gamos*) as the highest form of physical and spiritual pleasure. In doing so, he cheapens the luxurious experience God intended for us.

Is the Church Anti-Sex?

Throughout history, sexual activity has been a difficult subject for churches to respond to. The typical pastor caring for his flock would often encounter the results of inappropriate sexual expression, and then be charged with cleaning up the mess. Sexual immorality has widespread results, affecting many in its wake. Even the apostle Paul had to confront a sexually destructive situation as shepherd of the church in Corinth, where a man was sleeping with his stepmother. It is no wonder that some pastors may, at times, wish that God had not given us such strong libidos.

But does this mean that the church is anti-sex? According to *The Da Vinci Code*, the church is the grand oppressor of sex. Brown says that "the natural sexual union between man and woman through which each became spiritually whole ... had been recast as a shameful act" (125). Recast by whom? According to Brown, it was the Catholic church's doing. But why?

The *why*, says Brown, was to "'reeducate' the pagan and feminine-worshipping religions" (125). Robert Langdon explains it to Sophie:

> "For the early church," Langdon explained in a soft voice, "mankind's use of sex to commune directly with God posed a serious threat to the Catholic power base. It left the Church out of the loop, undermining their self-proclaimed status as the *sole* conduit to God. For obvious reasons, they worked hard to demonize sex and recast it as a disgusting and sinful act. Other major religions did the same" (309).

Brown draws heavily from a handful of other books for the theories presented by his characters in the novel. One of these books is *The Templar Revelation*, written by occultists Lynn Picknett and Clive Prince. Picknett and Prince seem to have influenced Brown's thinking about God and sex:

> Sex was—and in many cases still is—deemed only acceptable between those whose unions are likely to result in procreation. For this reason, there is no Christian concept of sex for joy only, let alone the idea—as in Tantrism or alchemy—that it can bring spiritual enlightenment.[2]

Is Brown correct in his assessment of the church's view of sex? Does he accurately portray the historical Christian view of sex? The answer to the question is resoundingly more complex than *The Da Vinci Code* would have us believe.

While the Bible extols the joys and delights of marital sexual expression, some of the early church leaders immediately after the biblical period (A.D. 100) wrote in response to the cultural influences and conflicting understanding of their day.

- Historic religious paganism advocated gross unrestrained sexual chaos, with which *The Da Vinci Code* is enamored.

- Some Christians overreacted and placed an undue premium on asceticism, a call for rigorous self-denial. Thus some of the early church fathers defended virginity or celibacy instead of marriage.

- In violation of the biblical mandate, some early church leaders embraced the idea of continence within marriage: the idea that one would be married, yet refrain from sexual expression.

- Some taught that sexual expression between a husband and wife should be only for purposes of procreation as opposed to the oneness and joy that accompanies biblical marital sexual expression.

To varying degrees, all of these views contradict or compromise the biblical position that sexual intercourse between a husband and wife is a righteous act.

Some of the early writers on the topic were conflicted. In

his prolific writings, Augustine vacillated (in part because he was so filled with regret about his own pre-Christian immorality) between a condemning tone regarding sexual expression and strong affirmations of the role of marriage. Some of the early church fathers wrote glowingly about the value of marriage, stating that within marriage, the couple partnered with God in creation. Julian of Eclanum, who carried on a vigorous debate with Augustine on the topic, expressed a distinctively biblical theme—that sexual expression between a husband and wife was intrinsically good since it was created by God.

> The Da Vinci Code *asserts that the church is the grand oppressor of sex.*

WAS SEX THE "ORIGINAL SIN"?

The Da Vinci Code paints an inaccurate picture of the portrayals of sexuality in the early church. Sweeping categorizations mislead the reader regarding the wide range of opinions that emerged from a large group of thinkers and writers—separated from each other by geography and often by centuries—who were responding to the sexual chaos of paganism on one hand, and to the excesses of rigorous asceticism on the other.

One example of Brown's inaccurate representation is Langdon's statement equating the sex act with "original sin." Once again, he selects the aberration and makes it the norm. A handful of the early church fathers did mistakenly believe that original sin was the sex act itself, but by far most did not,

ASCETICISM —AVOIDANCE
PAGANISM — INDULGENCE

despite what *The Da Vinci Code* would have us believe (125). And even though certain church fathers seem to have had a view of sex that did not match the Bible's teaching of maximum sexual fulfillment, their motivation could just as well have been sincerely (though misguided) for the spiritual well-being of their flocks. Arbitrarily and summarily assigning them the motive of politics and trying to control others is logically flawed and a stereotyped generalization.

SEX AS THE "DIVINE MOMENT"

Surprisingly, *The Da Vinci Code* is accurate in one of its portrayals of sexual expression. Brown is correct in describing the "divine-ness" or "divinity" of the sex act. He contends that it is in sexual union that God is experienced (308). But he is not correct for the reasons he believes.

The Bible explains clearly why sexual union is a divine moment for a husband and a wife. When God created males, He created entities that were only a partial explanation of who God is. When God created females, likewise, they were only a partial expression of the fullness of God's nature. Yet we are told that we are created in the image of God (see Genesis 1:26–27). How can this be true when we consider that males tend to identify most readily with the distinctly masculine components of God, while at the same time, females tend to identify with the feminine descriptors for God?

The God of the Bible, though called our heavenly Father, has no gender—He has no genitalia, no X or Y chromosomes. God is spirit (see John 4:24), and the mystery of His Person goes way beyond anything we humans can imagine. It is in that sense—in terms of His spiritual nature—that the Bible describes us as created "in his image" (Genesis 1:27). He is the Person from whom our "personness" is derived, both male and female.

That's not to say that God is a mix of human maleness and human femaleness. We can't describe Him as androgynous. God created male and female genders; they don't define Him. And while He created us "male and female" for a number of reasons, one was certainly to express in the created universe some diverse elements that reflect His own character. So even while the Bible most often refers to God by masculine names and pronouns (such as "Father" and "he"), sometimes he is compared to a mother holding a newborn or to a hen guarding her chicks (see Matthew 23:37; Isaiah 49:15).

A male by himself is a partial representative of who God is. A female by herself is a partial representative of the spectrum of God's characteristics. When a man and a woman come together sexually in "one flesh" (Genesis 2:24), they become a more complete expression of the spectrum of God's characteristics. This is a crucial aspect of the amazing power—the indescribable magnetism—of sex. It is meant to be a response to the potent stamp on the core of our beings—a more complete expression of the infinite spectrum of God's characteristics.

Our sexuality and our spirit are profoundly intertwined.

It is this spiritual dimension of the pleasure and pull of

sexual expression that sanctifies sex. The result of the male-female union is not some androgynous entity. Men remain spectacularly male and masculine. Women remain wonderfully female and feminine. Unlike paganism's fascination with androgyny, the Bible affirms fully the magnificent differences of maleness and femaleness.

GOD'S GUIDE TO MAXIMUM SEX

Our sexuality and our spirit are inexplicably and profoundly intertwined. We are—at our core—spirit beings, created in God's image. So our sexuality is likewise at that same core—it must be, because we are more than animals in our nature. (If sexuality were merely physical, then God should have included male and female animals as created in His image.) That is why sexuality cannot be perceived as some mere tangent for us humans, as if it were something removed from our spirit. That is also why it is so serious to tamper with the sexual part of our beings, whether by sexual things done *by* us, or sexual things done *to* us. And that is why sexual behavior such as homosexuality, bestiality, pedophilia, and transsexuality are so harmful, and an offense to God. All of these, in their unique ways, tarnish the full representation of the image of God that defines us.

But in order for the act of sexual expression between a man and woman to be fully representative of the spectrum of the characteristics of God, a male and female must be one in totality—and that includes oneness not merely physically, but oneness emotionally, spiritually, and psychologically. That oneness is not something experienced for a moment—it

is lifelong. There is a phrase for this unique unity of being—
it is called the covenant of marriage.

Protecting a Good Thing

God is so thoroughly pro-sex that He has established
boundaries by which to protect it, to maximize its joy. Since
He designed sex and sexual expression, He knows what
works and what doesn't. He knows what brings short-term
delight but long-term pain. In contrast, He also knows what
will bring long-term delight. Consequently, God has designed
ways by which to express this spectacular gift in order to
bring the utmost delight.

Those protectors are (1) heterosexuality and (2)
monogamy. Heterosexuality represents the completeness
that results from the fit between male and female. It does not
require deep insight to understand how males and females
fit together. And when these differing anatomies come
together, they are able to produce results that other forms of
sexual expression (homosexuality, pornography, bestiality,
and so forth) cannot. Monogamy is required to provide the
security of enduring, growing, developing, nurtured,
authentic love. This love stands in stark contrast to the
throw-away, who-looks-the-best-for-the-moment type of
lust that results in multiple partners and deep emotional
pain and rejection.

There is a land within these boundaries where two people
can live and enjoy sexual fulfillment to its utmost. It is called
marriage. And we're not talking just any marriage. This promised land is the biblically based, "one-flesh" marriage.

The "One-Flesh" Marriage

In the first chapter of Genesis, the term "it was good" appears six different times. When God created humankind, He declared that "it was very good" (v. 31) . Not just good, but "*very* good." But in Genesis 2:18, the phrasing changes: "it is *not* good." After all the "goods," why does a "*not* good" suddenly appear? Simply stated, man was not designed to be alone. God Himself is not alone—He wouldn't be, even if there were no other created beings in existence. That's because He is a father, a son, and a spirit. "Father, Son, and Holy Spirit" is not merely a benediction in a religious service. It is, above all, a profound statement of His own self-contained "community," or "relationship." God Himself is "in" relationship. We were made with His stamp on us. We, too, are created with a need for relationship.

God is so thoroughly "pro-sex" that He has established boundaries to protect it.

Thus God made humanity with the need for community, for relationship. And He further satisfied that need for deep intimacy in a spectacular way through the coming together of a husband and wife physically, emotionally, and spiritually in the sex act. *That* is maximum sex. God's will was that male and female would become "one flesh" (Genesis 2:24); that is, truly "one" in every way: physically, psychologically, emotionally, intellectually, and spiritually.

Mentally and emotionally, a monogamous relationship is

healthy. A recent Ohio State University study shows that marriage is good for mental health, as well as for sexual benefits. Sociologists discovered "that over a five-year period, getting married or staying married alleviated the symptoms of depression much more than being single, divorced or cohabiting. Remarriage also improved mental health, but not as much as first marriage. Even unhappily married depressives fared better than singles."[3]

It's no mistake that marriage is emotionally healthful. God designed the covenant of marriage as a profound security for individuals. Not surprisingly, sexual fulfillment is best experienced in the context of a secure, lifelong relationship. And that is one of the great tragedies of Robert Langdon's legitimizing the anti-biblical pagan understanding of reality. Ultimately it hurts people—badly; not just sexually, but in every aspect of their lives.

GOD'S SECOND BEST IDEA

I (Jim) pastor a wonderful church in the San Diego area. I also travel and speak at various conferences, and have authored several books. But it is quite possible that one single sentence I wrote has given me more visibility than all of my books combined and, candidly, more visibility than I ever intended.

Some years ago I was asked to send in some quotes to be included in a small book. I sent approximately twenty quotes to the author. Months passed. I forgot about the book project.

Then one day, I received by mail the little paperback book of quotes. I quickly glanced through it to see if the author had included any of my statements. After skimming through the book several times, I concluded that none of my quotes had "made the cut." I was almost ready to lay the book down when I saw my name on a page. There, above my name, in big, bold print, occupying an entire page (as all the quotes did), I read these words: *Sex is God's idea, and second to salvation, it's the best idea He ever had.* Frankly, I was a bit shocked. Of all the quotes I had sent in, this is the only one that made it into the little book of sayings. I was a bit horrified, thinking that all I would be remembered for in all of history is a statement about sex.

At that moment my two oldest children—who were teenagers at the time—walked into the room. They wanted to see what I was reading. When they saw that their dad would be remembered for a statement about sex, they burst out laughing. They thought it was hilarious.

My response was, "No, I won't be remembered by this. Nobody will even see it. Nobody will ever read this little book." That did not stop their laughter. They were delighted to see me squirming a bit—especially on the topic of sex.

A month or two passed. I had once again forgotten this sentence. Then one day I was flipping through a magazine, and there in the left-hand margin, for all the world to see, was my sex quote. Within a month or so, it appeared in another magazine. By that time some of my friends across the country were seeing it, tearing out the pages from the magazines and mailing them to me. One of them summarized it this way: "Jim, you have entirely too much free time on your hands!"

As the years have passed, I have learned to "wear my quote" as a badge of honor. Why? Because it's true. Sex *is* God's idea, and second to salvation, it *is* the best idea He ever shared with us. I am glad I wrote that sentence, if even just to remind myself of this wonderful gift God gave to us. He certainly is not ashamed of His gift!

"The Code"—even the portion pertaining to sex— if left unchallenged, systematically deletes a portion of the Divine Arc.

—◆—

CHAPTER 3

Is it true that there was a matriarchal culture that the church attempted to crush?

Is it true that the church hunted down and killed more than five million women over three centuries as part of a brutal "reeducation" (125)?

Is it true that the church, even today, seeks to demonize and repress women?

Is it true that "Jesus was the original feminist" (248)?

And if this section of the code is left unchallenged,
another piece of the Divine Arc is removed.

WOMEN ARE MORE SACRED AND FEMININE THAN THE "SACRED FEMININE"

"… Constantine and his male successors successfully converted the world from matriarchal paganism to patriarchal Christianity by waging a campaign of propaganda that demonized the sacred feminine, obliterating the goddess from modern religion forever" (124).

"Why can't I wear a dress to the party?" whined nine-year-old Carrie.

"Because dresses are for girls," replied Nancy Williams, unwrapping her next pack of cigarettes.

"But I *am* a girl!" cried Carrie.

"No, you're not. You've outgrown that. Now you are a young woman. And women no longer have to wear dresses. They can wear whatever they like." Her rough voice did not match her features, which most would call beautiful.

"Okay, well, I like dresses." Carrie was already showing the stubborn streak she had inherited from her mother. "And if I can wear anything I like, I want to wear my pink dress with the seashells on it."

Her mother put down the freshly lit smoke and turned toward her daughter, trying to keep her temper in check. "Carrie, do you know what Women's Liberation means?"

Carrie shook her head. She didn't understand the term, but somehow she knew it would mean she couldn't wear her favorite dress to the party.

"Women's Liberation," continued her mother, "is all about freeing women from hundreds—thousands—of years of being told what to do by men. It is hundreds of thousands of women standing up all around the world saying, 'We are women. We are not slaves to men.' Being a woman means you don't have to wear dresses just to impress boys. You can wear jeans and sneakers just like they do."

"But I'm not a slave, Mama. I'm just nine. And I like to wear dresses. They make me feel pretty and—"

"You only think they make you feel pretty 'cause that's what men have made you think. Liberated women make up their own minds about what 'pretty' is. We don't need men to make up our minds for us."

Carrie looked up at her mother and asked in a quiet voice, "Is that why Daddy doesn't live with us anymore? Because you're 'liberated' and don't need him?"

Nancy Williams picked up her cigarette from the ashtray and took a long drag before answering. "That's right, Carrie. Your father liked me okay when I did everything the way he wanted. When I learned I could think for myself, he got mad and left. You see, he just didn't like a woman who thinks for herself."

Carrie blinked several times to bring herself back to the present. Jen was leading tonight's discussion group on *The Da Vinci Code.* The phrase, "the dangers of freethinking women" from page 125 of the book had taken her back nearly fifteen years into her childhood. Jen had read that passage to lead into this night's discussion, So Dark the Con of Man.

"Five million women were tortured and murdered by the church over a period of three hundred years. Five million women!"

"But how could people let that happen?" asked Amanda. Carrie knew Amanda from their freshman year when they had taken a course in world history together. "I mean, wouldn't decent people have protested? Surely there would have been some sort of backlash."

Heads nodded in unison to this question.

"Ah," said Jen, a shrewd smile on her face. "Therein lies the Dark Con of Man. It was the church, made up of the very people you would think would rise up and stop this kind of madness, that was carrying out the systematic executions. The church convinced its gullible followers that if a woman showed any kind of intelligence—if she knew how to heal a wound, for instance; or if she could solve a math equation—she must be a witch. The church was terribly afraid of losing its power to women who happened to be smarter than it was.

"It's just like Langdon says here on page 124: '… powerful men in the early Christian church "conned" the world by propagating lies that devalued the female and tipped the scales in favor of the masculine.' That's the Dark Con of Man."

Amanda spoke up again. "And listen to what Langdon says later on the same page: 'The Priory believes that Constantine and his male successors successfully converted the world from matriarchal paganism to patriarchal Christianity by waging a campaign of propaganda that demonized the sacred feminine, obliterating the goddess from modern religion forever.'"

Wow, thought Carrie. *So that's who started the oppression of women: the church.* The Da Vinci Code was helping her to make sense of her Women's Studies classes. She couldn't wait to get back to her dorm to read more.

———⊰•⊱———

All the subtlety of *The Da Vinci Code* disappears each time the topic of women is mentioned. Brown's thesis is succinct: *Christianity destroyed and killed women. Paganism affirmed them.* But he is wrong. Very wrong. If ever a book should be written off as "mere fiction," *The Da Vinci Code* is the one.

On the other hand, this book can't be ignored so easily. Due to its author's effective sprinkling of occasional "facts," along with assertions by the characters that they are speaking the truth, Brown's book is neither fact nor fiction. It is "fact-ion"— that is, a wily narrative that blends limited facts with some grossly exaggerated claims (like the claim that the church killed five million women in its witch hunts); these claims are placed in the unfolding plot in real locations and times to provide sufficient plausibility. The result is a stunning and effective propaganda piece that moves its readers to a skewed perception of reality.

> *The novel's thesis is succinct:*
>
> *Christianity destroyed and killed*
>
> *women. Paganism affirmed them.*

Our first impression of *The Da Vinci Code* was, "It won't be taken seriously; after all, it is just fiction." We were wrong. We assumed people would know that the book is fiction and take it as such. But in its "faction" form, it has become a powerful advocate for a code that has significant real-life implications for you today.

Is it true that the church, even today, seeks to demonize and repress women?

Is it true that there was a matriarchal culture that the church attempted to crush?

Is it true that the church hunted down and killed more than five million women over three centuries as part of a brutal "reeducation" (125)?

Is it true that the church, even today, seeks to demonize and repress women?

Is it true that Jesus was the original feminist (248)?

The signs of this code, or at least the portion we are concerned with in this chapter, are neither new nor impressive: Brown makes some sweeping accusations about how the church (or persons representing the church) denigrates women, treating them as accomplices of Satan. Then he creates a gender-fueled conspiracy and manipulates reality in order to demonstrate that pagan female cultures were much better than our Judeo-Christian cultures today. In doing so, Brown conveniently ignores the biblical view of women.

DID CHRISTIANITY CONSPIRE TO SUBJUGATE WOMEN?

We are not saying that Brown is completely wrong in writing that women have, at times, been mistreated by those who claim to be Christians. At the same time, we object to Brown's technique of focusing on the aberrations while ignoring normative, biblically based Christianity.

As Christians, we sadly acknowledge that there are sins within the church on this issue. And those sins cannot be simply swept under the carpet. We acknowledge that the church is comprised of broken, and often sinful, people. While speaking to a large congregation, I (Jim) once asked, "Is there any man here who has not, at some time, taken advantage of a woman, or at least mistreated a woman, in *some* way?" No one raised his hand. We were all guilty.

The Matriarchy Myth

Brown writes, "Constantine and his male successors successfully converted the world from matriarchal paganism to patriarchal Christianity" (124). He wishfully imagines a matriarchal time before patriarchal rule.

We acknowledge that the church is comprised of broken, often sinful, people.

Before we consider his claims against Christianity, let us examine the question of patriarchal versus matriarchal in the entire scope of history. All history, including secular as well as biblical history, is more *male*-led than *female*-led. In spite of the fact that there have been many superb female leaders in both secular as well as in biblical and Christian history, the preponderance of leaders has been men.

Regarding this issue of former matriarchal societies, Steven Goldberg, chairman of the Department of Sociology at City College, City University of New York, wrote,

> The point is that authority and leadership are, and always have been, associated with the male in every society, and I refer to this when I say that patriarchy is universal and that there has never been a matriarchy ... Theories that hypothesized a matriarchal form of society at "an earlier stage of history" made a certain, if tortuous sense, until the findings of the past 50 years failed to include a single shred of evidence that such matriarchies had ever existed and demonstrated the inability of all such theories to deal with reality. [Of the h]undreds of the societies we have studied in this century ... Without exception [they] have been patriarchal ... [Margaret] Mead acknowledged that "It is true ... that all the claims so glibly made about societies ruled by women are nonsense. We have no reason to believe that they ever existed."[1]

Goldberg's contentions are clear. There is not a "single shred of evidence" to show female-led early civilizations. Men, according to noted anthropologist Margaret Mead, "everywhere have been in charge of running the show." These are two highly-regarded scholars saying there never has been such a thing as a matriarchal society. How then, if it never existed, was Constantine able to convert it to patriarchal rule?

Which Philosophy Truly Esteems Women?

Brown implies that pagan nations affirmed women. But does that square with reality? In truth, women in the ancient pagan world were not viewed or treated as well as Langdon would have Sophie believe.

In Alvin Schmidt's groundbreaking book, *Under the Influence: How Christianity Transformed Civilization,* we see that before the coming of Christ, when the world of paganism was dominant, the lives of most women were held in very low regard. In Greece, India, and China, women had no rights and were considered the property of their husbands. The Greek philosophers of the day had no higher view of women than did other non-Christians. Aristotle taught that a woman ranked somewhere between a man and a slave. Plato taught that if a man lived a cowardly life, he would be reincarnated as a woman.

In ancient Greece, women—especially wives—were regarded as lowly. A wife was not allowed to leave her house unescorted. She was not allowed to eat or interact with guests in the home, but was consigned to her quarters (*gynaeceum*). In contrast, a *hetaera* (mistress) was allowed to accompany a married man in public.[3]

The average Athenian woman had the social status of a slave. Women were not educated, nor were they allowed to speak in public. Silence was considered the great grace of a woman, even at home. Not only were women considered inferior, they were also thought to be the source of evil and were thus not to be trusted.

The advent of Christianity radically transformed the fate of women. Even ancient Roman pagan scholars agree that it was the turning point for the freedom and dignity of women.[2]

Before the coming of Christ, most women were held in low regard.

Wherever Christianity has been introduced, it has lifted up women, not just in antiquity but even in modern times. Sex-selection infanticide was common in 1880 in pagan China before the influence of Christian missionaries. Girl babies were disposed of as a liability. In the last two centuries, because of Christian influences, the treatment of women worldwide has improved immensely. It was the influence of Christians that helped to abolish China's practice of binding women's feet in order to create the diminutive effect that men found attractive. This dangerous practice had led to gangrene infection, needless amputation, and sometimes even death.

In India, the practice of *suttee* was ended by the influence of Christianity. A good Hindu wife was expected to follow her husband in death on the funeral pyre, even if she was young with her whole life ahead of her. "Child widows" were also part of the pagan goddess-worshiping Hindu culture. These girls were raised to be temple prostitutes. Amy Carmichael, a Christian, fought to put an end to this practice by rescuing girls from it.

THE GREAT EUROPEAN WITCH HUNT

Nevertheless, Brown paints a completely different picture through his characters in *The Da Vinci Code*. According to Professor Langdon, Christianity is violently anti-woman. Langdon recounts the atrocities of the Middle Ages, an era known as the "Great Hunt" or simply, "The Burning." Langdon recalls how the Catholic church, fueled by a publication titled *Malleus Maleficarum*, or *The Witches' Hammer*, began a crusade against any woman deemed a threat to the church's power base, labeling such a woman a witch.

> Those deemed "witches" by the Church included all female scholars, priestesses, gypsies, mystics, nature lovers, herb gatherers, and any women "suspiciously attuned to the natural world."
> … During three hundred years of witch hunts, the Church burned at the stake an astounding five *million* women (125).

Brown has based his claims on old research that has been proven unreliable and deliberately misleading. Jenny Gibbons, in an article titled "Recent Developments in the Study of The Great European Witch Hunt," writes, "Many articles in Pagan magazines contain almost no accurate information about the 'Burning Times,' primarily because we rely so heavily on out-dated research."[4]

She goes on to insist, "If your knowledge of the 'Burning Times' is based on popular or Pagan literature, nearly everything you know may be wrong."[5]

For instance, Brown refers to *Malleus Maleficarum* as being authored by an official of the Catholic church. Actually, the church reacted to its publication by rejecting the legal procedures suggested by the authors, and censuring them a few years later. It was secular courts, not the church, that relied on *Malleus Maleficarum.*

Secular courts, not church courts, handed down the majority of capital sentences. Those found guilty of witchcraft by the church were usually given nonlethal penalties, such as excommunication, or fasting on bread and water for a year.

"Popular writers," says Gibbons, "trumpeted that the Great Hunt was not a mere panic, but a deliberate attempt to exterminate Christianity's rival religion."[6] This is what Brown would have us believe. It is what he means when he refers to the "brutal crusade to 'reeducate' the pagan and feminine-worshipping religions" (125).

Gibbons continues: "Today, we know that there is absolutely no evidence to support this theory. When the church was at the height of its power (11th to 14th centuries) very few witches died. Persecutions did not reach epidemic levels until after the Reformation, when the Catholic church had lost its position as Europe's indisputable moral authority."[7]

It was Christian missionaries who encouraged kingdoms and courts to pass laws protecting men and women from charges of witchcraft. These missionaries said such charges were ungrounded, as they did not believe humans possessed the power to do what witches were accused of doing. "For example," writes Gibbons, "the fifth century *Synod of St. Patrick* ruled that 'A Christian who believes that there is a vampire in the world, that is to say, a witch, is to be anathematized; whoever lays that reputation upon a living being shall not be received into the Church until he revokes with his own voice the crime that he has committed.'"[8]

And what of the estimates of the number of women killed during the Great Hunt? The estimated number of those killed ranges from hundreds of thousands to nine million. Brown uses the figure of five million. But again, modern research reveals that this is not the case.

"On the wilder shores of the feminist and witch-cult movements," writes Robin Briggs, a scholar at Oxford University, "a potent myth has become established, to the effect that nine million women were burned as witches in Europe; gendercide rather than genocide. This is an overestimate by a factor of up to 200, for most reasonable modern estimates suggest perhaps 100,000 trials between 1450 and 1750, with something between 40,000 and 50,000 executions, of which 20 to 25 percent were men."[9] Gibbons refers to two other scholars, Brian Levack and Ronald Hutton, who agree with Briggs's number of those who were actually put to death for witchcraft. Even so, scholars Ross Clifford and Philip Johnson aptly voice the sentiment of most biblically consistent Christians: "That was 40,000 casualties too many ... the Inquisition and Salem trials were a hideous violation of human dignity and utterly inexcusable."[10] Indeed, while the number of so-called witches burned has been wildly exaggerated, Christians must concede that the burning of even one person is indefensible.

Gibbons concludes her essay by saying, "We Neopagans

now face a crisis. As new data appeared, historians altered their theories to account for it. We have not. Therefore an enormous gap has opened between the academic and the 'average' Pagan view of witchcraft … We avoid the somewhat dull academic texts that present solid research, preferring sensational writers who play to our emotions."[11]Gibbons wrote this in 1998, nearly five years before the publication of *The Da Vinci Code*. She is a self-confessed Pagan who is concerned about writers using misleading information to cast the church in a negative light in reference to the Great Hunt.

THE TRUTH ABOUT THE BIBLE'S ESTEEM OF WOMEN

If Dan Brown had wanted to use reliable information for his research into how Christians view women, he need not have gone any further than the Bible. Consider the examples from the Old Testament.

In Genesis, we learn that both males and females receive their identity, their sense of value, from their relationship with the Creator, being made in the image of God (Genesis 1:27).

The Da Vinci Code repeatedly misquotes the Bible, stating that Eve ate the fruit; thus she, the first female, brought sin into the world. However, in Genesis 2, which provides more detail regarding creation than Genesis 1, the instruction not to eat the fruit was given to the male, Adam, before the female was created (Genesis 2:16–18, 22). The primary disobedience in Genesis 3 was the failure of the *male* to give protection, leadership, and nurture to his home. This was not merely a *woman's* sin. This was, first of all, a *man's* sin. Cowardly Adam tries to shift the blame to Eve ("the woman," Genesis 3:12) and even to God ("whom you gave me," Genesis 3:12). Eve was an accomplice. That is why God confronts both of them (Genesis 3:9–19).

The apostle Paul states it even more emphatically. He says that sin entered the world through the actions of one *man*, Adam (Romans 5:17).

Exalted Women of the Old Testament

Consider more examples of how women are portrayed in the Old Testament.

Esther was courageous to the point of defying the king himself, an action that usually resulted in death. The outcome of her courage was the salvation of an entire race of people (Esther 1–10).

Ruth was loyal, astute, and shrewd. She stayed with her impoverished mother-in-law after the death of Ruth's husband. She humbled herself in order to secure food for herself and her mother-in-law. And she was obedient, marrying a stranger who ended up loving and caring for Ruth and her family (Ruth 1–4).

Deborah was a wife, mother, and judge in Israel (Judges 4).

Proverbs 31 affirms the greatness of women, demonstrating their ability to juggle the amazing pressures as community leaders, businesswomen, wives, and mothers. The chapter exalts the qualities of one whom the Bible portrays as a model woman:

- She is skilled with her hands (vv. 13, 19) and her mind (vv. 13–31).

- She understands manufacturing (vv. 13, 24); importing (v. 14); time management (v. 15); real estate investing (v. 16); agribusiness (v. 16); physical workouts (v. 17); business profit (vv. 16, 18, 24); a work ethic (vv. 15, 18); "hands on" labor (v. 19); welfare and compassion (v. 20); planning, administration, and organization (v. 21); and fashion (vv. 21–22).

- When she speaks, she is articulate and her speech is content-rich (v. 26).

- She is an instructor, a teacher (v. 26).

- She is an unashamed homemaker—and a good one (v. 27).

- Not surprisingly, she is busy—very busy (v. 27).

- She enjoys being a mother and is quite successful in child rearing (v. 28).

Does this sound like a repressed woman?

Exalted Women of the New Testament: the Genealogy of Jesus

The New Testament begins with "the genealogy of Jesus Christ" (Matthew 1:1–16). If the fictional Robert Langdon is correct, the New Testament was manipulated into being by a group of female-bashing chauvinists. If that is so, then why would these male elitists allow women to have a prominent role in the genealogy, a most unusual inclusion considering that a typical lineage at that time would have included only males? If the early leaders of Christianity were as villainous as *The Da Vinci Code* states, then no women would have been included. But five were. Who were these five women?

- Tamar—a twice-widowed woman who had sexual relations with her father-in-law—was the first woman to be mentioned (Genesis 38:11–30).

- Rahab was a prostitute in the city of Jericho (Joshua 2:1).

- Ruth was a woman with a sterling character (Ruth 2:11).

- The wife of Uriah, Bathsheba, is remembered as the woman with whom King David had an affair (2 Samuel 11:1–27).

- The final woman in the genealogy of Christ is, predictably, Mary, the mother of Jesus (Matthew 1:16). Presumably between the ages of thirteen and fifteen, in a small community, Mary became pregnant—before marriage and, miraculously, without having had sexual intercourse. The Virgin Birth is a core doctrine of the Christian faith, but what is important to note is that the role of the mother was so honored as to be cited in a list that would typically include only the father.

If the church through the ages had been as anti-female as Professor Langdon and Leigh Teabing told Sophie, then most certainly it would have deleted such female-honoring passages from the Scriptures.

And the examples don't stop with Mary, Jesus' mother.

More Exalted Women of the New Testament

Jesus' very first announcement that He was the Messiah was shared with a woman, and not just any woman. She was a five-time divorcee, involved with a live-in boyfriend.

Furthermore, she was a Samaritan, which meant that Jesus violated the mores of the time by crossing racial lines (John 4:17–26).

When Mary (the sister of Martha and Lazarus) listened to Jesus' teachings (at that time an activity reserved for males) and Martha scurried about fulfilling the "female" role, Jesus affirmed Mary and challenged Martha (Luke 10:41–42).

In contrast to the custom of the time, a group of women were part of the entourage that traveled with Jesus and other men. These women even supported His ministry financially (Luke 8:1–3).

In the book of Acts, Peter cites an Old Testament scripture saying that both "your sons and daughters will prophesy" (Joel 2:28).

Paul, who is so often accused by feminists of being anti-woman, uses forceful language to declare that both sexes have equal standing before Christ. Neither males nor females have precedent in God's eyes (Galatians 3:28).

Following the often-discussed directive wives, submit to your husbands (Ephesians 5:22), Paul, only three verses later, gives the most

THE GOSPEL OF THOMAS

The Da Vinci Code would have us believe that the Gnostic Gospels affirmed women, where the New Testament put women down. Yet this passage from the Gnostic Gospel of Thomas gives us a different picture.

Gnostic Misogyny

Simon Peter said to them: "Let Mary [probably Magdalene] leave us, for women are not worthy of life." Jesus said, "I myself shall lead her in order to make her male, so that she too may become a living spirit, resembling your males. For every woman who will make herself male will enter the kingdom of heaven" (Gospel of Thomas, saying 114).

difficult assignment any male has ever received: "Husbands, love your wives, just as Christ loved the church and gave himself up for her"(Ephesians 5:25). In other words, a husband is to give up his life for his wife.

We must not forget that the Bible gives a massive endorsement to the countless faceless women who never assumed public roles, but nevertheless faithfully served God in the essential role of mother and wife.

The single strongest affirmation of women in the New Testament is found in the fact that a woman—who, according to the customs of the time, would not have been allowed to testify in court—is the one to testify regarding the single most important announcement in all of biblical or Christian history: the actual, literal, physical resurrection of Jesus from the dead (Matthew 28:1; Mark 16:1; Luke 24:10). All of Christianity hinges on this one event, and a woman was chosen for this highest honor.

In light of the evidence cited above, we submit that anyone who claims the Holy Bible is intended to repress women has not read the Bible very carefully. On the contrary, it tells us that God holds women in high esteem, and thus, so should Christians everywhere.

WOMEN IN THE EARLY CHURCH

Brown also asserts, "[P]owerful men in the early Christian church 'conned' the world by propagating lies that devalued the female and tipped the scales in favor of the masculine" (124). Is this true?

While the Bible itself, and Jesus personally, upheld a high

respect for women, it must be acknowledged that there were anti-women statements from church leaders—Tertullian, Cyril of Jerusalem, Jerome, and Augustine as examples—during the third through fifth centuries. Some of these continued through persons such as Thomas Aquinas and others, even past the Reformation. Such statements are contrary to the Bible and to Jesus. Those statements are an embarrassment to all Christians. And, thankfully, those statements are offset by volumes of strong affirmations of women, and by the massive number of females who have ministered so effectively throughout the centuries of Christianity.

The writings of the early church fathers can be taken affirmatively or negatively, depending upon what one wishes to extract. Examples of writings that show gender equality would include:

- Clement of Alexandria: "Woman does not possess one nature, and man, another. Rather, they have the same."[12]
- Cyprian: "The mercy of Christ ... was equally divided among everyone—without difference of sex, ... years, ... persons.[13]

Admittedly, other writers of this age were less affirming. Some early writings blamed women for the inability of men to control their sexual desires. Other writers even insisted that women should confine themselves to childbearing and maintenance of the home. To deny the existence of this stream of thought would be less than honest.

However, present-day radical feminism has been obsessed with such statements, aggrandizing them and developing an entire feminist theology that insists early Christianity was fundamentally misogynistic. Using such venomous language to describe early Christianity, as a whole, is a broad generalization to say the least, and historically dishonest. *The Da Vinci Code* perpetrates this inaccurate and misleading "woman-hating" claim.

SPECTACULAR CONTRIBUTIONS OF WOMEN IN CHURCH HISTORY

Furthermore, Brown seems unaware of the spectacular contributions of women throughout church history.

- Perpetua: This twenty-six-year-old mother of a newborn, along with her servant girl Felicitas, demonstrated unequaled courage as they were martyred for their faith in March 205.

- Monica (331–387): She was the most significant influencer—as mother—on Augustine, one of the most influential persons of Christianity.

- Clare: Turning away from wealth to follow Christ, she established in 1212 the "Poor Clares," now located in seventy-six countries.

- Catherine of Sienna: Born in 1347, she was an activist, prayer leader, humanitarian, and adviser and counselor to the most powerful political and ecclesiastical leaders.

- Katherina von Bora: Without her, Martin Luther could never have become the leader of the Protestant Reformation in the 1500s.

- Susanna Wesley: The twenty-fifth child in her family, she gave birth to nineteen children, was a brilliant thinker, and theologian, and was the counselor, confidante, and theological mentor of son John Wesley, leader of the massive Evangelical Awakening in the 1700s.

- Catherine Booth: A stronger preacher than her husband William, she cofounded with him the Salvation Army in the late 1800s in England.

These women were strong. They were leaders. They were respected. And they were all part of the inexpressible contribution of women in Christian history.

But if Robert Langdon is correct, then there would be no record of women in the church's history. Women in the ministry, if the premise of *The Da Vinci Code* is correct, would have disappeared because of the oppression of "Constantine and his male successors." If da Vinci's code is truly in effect, then what do we make of these women just mentioned?

Perhaps a more significant question is this: If Brown is correct, if the

These women were strong.

They were leaders.

They were respected.

church has set out to systematically demonize the role of women in ministry, how do we account for all the great women throughout history, and in our lifetime, who have had such an incredible impact in the spiritual welfare of so many others?

WAS JESUS THE FIRST FEMINIST?

Males and females are gloriously different but unquestionably equal.

Christianity, as we have seen, strongly upholds women. The church, while fallible, has also taken great steps to protect and esteem women. So why are Christians and the church cast as anti-feminist?

The first women's rights conference in America was held in a Wesleyan church in 1848 in Seneca Falls, New York. On the 150th anniversary of this event, in 1998, there was a celebration of this conference. Yet in the national media coverage of that event, there was no mention of the church's role in the first conference. Perhaps that was because early feminism was *biblical* feminism based on the scriptural understanding of women: It is unrelated to today's radical pagan feminism.

Ironically, Brown's character Leigh Teabing was partially correct when he said, "Jesus was the original feminist" (248). Jesus, as we showed earlier, validated the role and value of women. Brown, however, recasts Jesus as a worshiper of Robert Langdon's paganistic "sacred feminine," a mockery of all recognized and credible research.

Jesus as the first feminist? Yes, if that means Jesus was always for the outcast, the forsaken, the mistreated, the hopeless. It was Jesus, not the pagan world that surrounded Him, who began to turn the tide in the way women are to be treated.

By treating women as equals, Jesus also criticized the evil of male chauvinism. And the same must be said of the apostles who followed Him. There is, however, one more thing we need to say. Jesus also knew that God the Creator, as the crowning of His work, created males and females to be different. This is the beautiful balance that the Bible seeks to maintain, which Jesus maintained—males and females gloriously different but unquestionably equal.

CHAUVINISM IS NOT HONORABLE

When Robin Morgan—the first radical feminist I (Jim) ever heard speak—came to Princeton Theological Seminary when I was a student there in the 1970s, she purposely ignored all males who raised their hands during the question-and-answer time. This, according to her, was so that "the sisterhood could experience power." This is the same woman who stated, "I feel that 'man-hating' is honorable."[14]

No, "man-hating" is not honorable. It is wrong. So is woman-hating. Chauvinism is wrong, whether it comes from men or from women. Women taking advantage of men are no better than men taking advantage of women. Both are wrong. Both are unbiblical. Both are un-Christian. *The Da Vinci Code* drives the gender wedge deeper, uplifting women at the expense of men, which is as offensive as uplifting men at the expense of women.

Brown brings out the worst in all of us with Sophie's innocent question, "You're saying the Christian church was to be carried on by a *woman*?" (248). No, the Christian church was not to be carried on by a *woman*. It is to be carried on by *both* men *and* women—persons, not separated by the culturally imposed restrictions of being male or female, but who instead embrace Jesus Christ (Galatians 3:28). The church was not and is not a "man's thing." Nor is it a "woman's thing." It is to be carried on by the people who follow God.

Contrary to *The Da Vinci Code*, the Bible, in particular, and Christianity, in general, are not anti-woman. In contrast, *The Da Vinci Code* expresses implicit and explicit anti-male sentiments.

What is driving Dan Brown's agenda? It is the pagan worldview that denies and distorts a core biblical truth: Men and women are created equal but different.

And if this section of the code is left unchallenged, another piece of the Divine Arc is removed.

CHAPTER 4

Is it true that Jesus' divinity was the result of a vote of bishops (233)?

Is it true that the early church hijacked Jesus' message and shrouded it with divinity (233)?

Is it true that Jesus was simply "a mortal prophet ... a great and powerful man, but a *man* nonetheless. A mortal" (233)?

If the code is left unchallenged when it denies the divinity of Jesus, another part of the Divine Arc is removed.

JESUS—WHO WAS HE, REALLY?

"Many scholars claim that the early Church literally stole Jesus from His original followers, hijacking His human message, shrouding it in an impenetrable cloak of divinity, and using it to expand their own power" (233).

Evan Taylor was exactly the kind of person Carrie should not have as a friend. Evan was intelligent (so he was probably afraid of a woman who threatened his intellect), confident (no doubt he manipulated women to do his bidding), and—worst of all—a Christian (among the original repressors of women). But somehow he and Carrie had become, if not close friends, at least friendly enough that they felt comfortable poking fun at one another.

"So you've fallen into the da Vinci trap, huh?" asked Evan easily as they walked back from the one class they shared, Conversational French. "Now every time you see the *Mona Lisa*, you're going to wonder if it really is the artist himself in drag." He said this in a gentle, mocking manner.

"I couldn't care less about those parts of the book," said Carrie, wondering why she felt it necessary to take a defensive position. "Da Vinci was, admittedly, an odd duck. What gets me is that what Christians believe about Jesus is all wrong; but I have a much clearer understanding of Jesus now, after reading Brown's book."

"So now Professor Langdon is teaching you theology, is he?"

"I wouldn't expect someone of your beliefs to accept the truth,"

Carrie shot back. "But it *is* true. You've elevated Jesus to god status, when that whole idea came as a result of a political maneuver by Constantine."

Evan, still smiling, replied, "I'm surprised at you, Carrie. Learning theology from a novel. Next you'll be telling me that you can prepare for the bar exam by reading Grisham."

Carrie thought on that for a moment, then started a new tack. "Well, what about this Council of Nicaea? You know, where Constantine voted Jesus divine. That's in a lot of theology books, not just *The Da Vinci Code*." She smiled, satisfied with her comeback.

"Well," said Evan, "I'll admit there was a Council of Nicaea, and you're right that Constantine was emperor at the time. Other than that ..."

"So," said Carrie, careful to keep her anger in check, "you're saying you still believe Jesus was divine?"

"Was and is," said Evan. "Remember, we Christians celebrate Easter—Christ risen from the dead."

Carrie walked along in silence for a while before responding. "But history is on Dan Brown's side, isn't it? I mean, did Jesus' followers think He was divine before the Council of Nicaea? And what about Constantine's vote? How can you really think someone who died two thousand years ago is still alive?"

Evan's smile spread across his face like the sunrise. "I'm glad you're asking these questions, Carrie. I really am. Here's a bench. Let's sit down and talk."

———

Just who was Jesus?

The answer to this question will not only shape the way you view *The Da Vinci Code*, but will ultimately shape your entire life. For, if Brown is correct in saying that Jesus was just a man, then our further debate with the author is meaningless. But if there is more to Jesus than Brown asserts, if Jesus truly is divine (with no help from Emperor Constantine), then we must also accept that what Jesus taught about life and eternity is true. Everything hangs on the answer to this question.

Is it true that Jesus' divinity was the result of a vote of bishops (233)?

Is it true that the early church hijacked Jesus' message and shrouded it with divinity (233)?

Is it true that Jesus was simply "a mortal prophet... a great and powerful man, but a *man* nonetheless. A mortal" (233)?

LIFE'S PIVOTAL QUESTION

Why were the followers of Jesus during His time on this earth so sure He was really divine? At what point did they come to that conclusion? On one occasion, Jesus asked His closest companions, "Who do people think I am?" (Matthew 16:13–20). This is a key moment in the life of Jesus. In contemporary language, the scene may have looked like this:

Jesus gathered His followers around Him one day and said, "Hey guys."

"Yes?" the disciples responded.

"You read the *Jerusalem Times'* Op-Ed piece, along with the letters to the editor. Who do they think I am?"

"Well, Jesus," one of them began, "some say that since You shed tears when You speak, You are old Jeremiah come back to life."

> *"Who do you say I am?"*
>
> —*Jesus*

Another one chimed in, "Yes, but others think that since You have done so many miracles, You are really Elijah come back to life."

"There's another theory floating around about You," another one stated, interrupting the previous disciple.

"And what is that?" Jesus asked.

"Well, since You preach really straight and direct, others think You are one of the prophet-preachers from seven hundred years ago come back to life."

"Very interesting," Jesus mused. "But what I really want to know is this: Who do *you guys* think I am?" It got quiet. Jesus had never put them on the spot like this before.

Peter spoke up first—as he often did. But this time he did not embarrass his friends. In fact, the blustery Peter was a bit low key. He started hesitatingly. "I know who You are!"

"Who?" Jesus asked gently.

"You are ..." Peter paused, then slowly completed the sentence, his confidence building, "... the Christ—the Messiah, the actual Son of God Himself!"

There was a long silence. Jesus stared intently at Peter, then at each of the other eleven close friends with him that day. They all knew the history of people claiming to be messiahs. During the four hundred years between the close of the Old Testament and the beginning of the New Testament, there were numerous individuals who claimed that they were the messiah. Each new messiah had raised the hopes of those who believed him. Then he had faded away. And with that supposed messiah went many broken hopes and dreams. So, was Jesus just another one? Would He disappear like all the rest?

After what seemed like a very long time, He finally spoke. "You're right, Peter. But you could not have learned that truth only from studying and reading the Old Testament. God, My Father, told you that in a direct, inspired way so that your word would be the rock of My church, declaring to the world who I really am."

He paused much longer this time. "So now," He said, "the word is out. You know who I am. And on *that* truth, on the reality that I *am the Christ, the Messiah—the Son of the Living God*—I am going to launch an unstoppable force. It will be called the church. It will be stronger than hell itself. But I must ask for a favor." His words just hung there. He didn't say anything more for a moment.

"Yes?" one of his friends said, wanting to break the silence.

"Do not tell anyone—at least not yet—that I am God, that I am Christ, that I am Messiah. Not yet."

What does Brown do with this conversation Jesus had with His disciples? What does he do with this rock upon which the church has been built for two thousand years? How does he respond to this essential truth today's followers of Christ hold most dear?

MERE MORTAL, OR MESSIAH?

Perhaps you are one of those readers who have been impressed by *The Da Vinci Code*'s case against biblical Christianity. Indeed, one must admit that if Jesus truly was merely a mortal man, and if this conversation we just read is false, then the heart is ripped out of the good news of Christianity and the Bible is not worth the paper it's written on.

But since we need all the good news we can get, we should hesitate before throwing out the good news of the Christian message, unless, of course, we have solid grounds for doing so. Answering *The Da Vinci Code*'s severe charge demands patience. Such a breathtaking, far-reaching generalization about Jesus will require responses in a number of following chapters, so stay with us and read on.

Let's begin by examining Brown's major assertion that "The early Church literally *stole* Jesus from His original followers, hijacking His human message, shrouding it in an impenetrable cloak of divinity … to expand their own power" (233).

To make sense of this claim we need to ask:

1. Who were "the original followers" that Brown names?
2. Where can we find this original "human message," and what is its content?
3. Who was part of "the early Church" who stole Jesus from these early followers?
4. When was this message distorted?
5. When was Jesus "shrouded in divinity"?

The Original "Gnostic" Followers

The Da Vinci Code makes a great deal of the discovery in 1945 of "secret scrolls," the so-called Nag Hammadi Gnostic texts. In chapter 7 we will look more closely at the influence of this discovery. For the moment, it is sufficient to know that Brown, following a marginal group of scholars who are committed to the undermining of biblical Christianity (particularly a group called the Jesus Seminar), argues that the "original disciples" were a group called Gnostics, not the writers of our New Testament.

Who were these Gnostics? In a nutshell, Gnostics were people who believed that every Christian was a "christ," and thus every Christian was "divine." Jesus was thus christ and divine only in this sense, not in any unique sense. Brown contends these Gnostic "original disciples" came before the men we associate as Jesus' disciples—Peter, James, John, and the rest. In order for Brown's theory to work, Peter and the rest of the New Testament disciples must have twisted the writings of the allegedly original Gnostic disciples.

Gnostics contend that the New Testament version of Jesus is a fabrication.

The Original Human Message

Their so-called human message is supposedly contained in one of these Gnostic texts called the Gospel of Thomas, as well as in a hypothetical document no one has ever seen called "Q." Both of these are claimed to predate the Gospels of the New Testament. In neither of these documents is there any teaching on the death, physical resurrection, and divine nature of Jesus, so Jesus is interpreted to be a human, though very spiritual, "guru" like the Buddha, concerned only with justice in this world. Are these documents reliable? We shall see.

Who Was in Brown's Early Church?

The later "early Church," according to Brown's theory, is made up of the apostles we all know—including Peter, John, Matthew, and Paul—who wrote the New Testament, imposing their later version of things on the original, human, Gnostic Jesus. From these apostles we get the "orthodox" Jesus, who died for the sins of the world, who rose from the dead, who left behind Him an empty tomb, and who was God in flesh. Gnostics say this version of Jesus is a fabrication.

If any historical person could identify what the original founders believed about Jesus, it was Paul.

According to modern scholars who hold to the Gnostic worldview, the alleged fabrication clearly took place when the "orthodox" Christians mentioned above wrote down their beliefs about Jesus in the biblical Gospels, suppressing the original texts and the true story of Jesus, specifically by making Him divine. This special sense of the term divine, as used by the church, meant that Jesus was the unique mediator between the transcendent divine Creator and sinful humanity—according to *The Da Vinci Code*, a lie.

We will deal with the case for "Q" and the Gospel of Thomas in chapter 7 where we show the unusually speculative character of this interpretation. We will examine the Gnostic beliefs in chapters 8 and 10 to show that they are a later perversion of original Christianity—indeed, its very opposite.

But even before we explore these topics in depth, we can see that Brown's explanation of the events of early Christianity runs out of time.

TIMING IS EVERYTHING

Our earliest Christian writings come from the pen of the apostle Paul, who wrote from around A.D. 48 to around A.D. 60. All recognized scholars and historians support this fact.[1] They agree Paul was a historical figure, a contemporary of Jesus, who, as a convinced rabbi, knew the early Christians well enough that he at first sought their extinction. In the late thirties he converted to Christianity, became a recognized Christian apostle, and finally was executed for his faith by Nero in A.D. 66. *There is no fact of early Christianity more historically verified and generally accepted by foes and friends alike.*

What is more, Paul's writings constitute the backbone of the New Testament. Since the life and ministry of Paul overlaps the historical beginnings of the Christian movement, he is the most historically dependable window into the faith of the earliest disciples of Jesus.

What scholars, such as those from the Jesus Seminar, and storytellers, such as Dan Brown, would have us believe is this: The "original Gnostic disciples" believed in a mortal (non-deity) Jesus. These disciples wrote their "gospels" portraying Jesus as a good man, a moral teacher, but not as divine. But these disciples somehow lost control of "their" Jesus to a group who took over (Brown uses the dramatic term "hijack[ed]") this growing sect called Christianity and completely reinterpreted the life, message, and mission of Jesus. This original group of Gnostics then disappeared without a trace until the middle of the second century.

Yet somehow, Paul, a prolific writer about Jesus and the church, never made mention of these "original Gnostic believers." The Gnostic argument is not serious history; it is a piece of fiction that cannot be substantiated.

The unimpeachable historicity of the apostle Paul and his writings completely undermines *The Da Vinci Code*'s view of things. Paul said that he depended on those who were apostles before him, and specifically named Peter, John, and James, Jesus' brother (1 Corinthians 9:5; Galatians 1:19; 2:8–9). He actually said, around A.D. 50, that he received from these men the original Gospel (1 Corinthians 15:3–5), again mentioning Peter and actually citing a text that came from the thirties that emphasized the absolute importance of Jesus' death and resurrection.[2] He called these men "pillars" (Galatians 2:9), that is, the foundational, eyewitness figures (1 Corinthians 15:5) on whom Jesus built the church (Matthew 16:15–18; Ephesians 2:20).

It is clear that the fourth century did not "invent" the divinity of Jesus.

If any historical person was in a position to identify what the original faith of the church was and what the original founders believed about Jesus, it was Paul. Paul said that what he preached was what these original founders preached (1 Corinthians 15:11).

In other words, what Paul preached was what the earliest church believed. As soon as we can nail down what Paul said about Jesus, we will know what the true original disciples believed about Jesus— which is not dependent on speculative theories but on solid history.

What did

Jesus teach

His disciples

about

Himself?

Shrouded in Divinity

When was Jesus shrouded in divinity? The simple answer is, from the beginning. The earliest disciples, as Paul shows, believed and taught that Jesus was a man, born from a human mother (Galatians 4:4). But in the same verse he called Jesus God's Son in the absolute sense of having a divine nature. Lest there be any doubt, Paul actually described Jesus as "being in very nature God" (Philippians 2:6). He wrote this early in the fifties. What is more, he cited a kind of hymn that is very Jewish and which doubtless goes back to the apostles in Palestine in the earliest days of the church (Philippians 2:5–11).

Add to these two texts from the earliest days of the church the mature statements of Paul about the divinity of Jesus—texts such as Romans 1:3 ("his [God's] Son"), 1 Corinthians 8:6 ("one Lord, Jesus Christ, through whom all things came"), and Colossians 1:15–16 ("He [Christ] is the image of the invisible God ... by him all things were created"), and it is clear that the fourth century did not invent the divinity of Jesus. The church in its earliest days held strongly to the belief that Jesus was completely and wholly divine in nature.

How Did Jesus View Himself?

If Paul is right, the Gospels are the earliest record of Jesus' earthly life. Paul knew Peter, James, and John, along with the other apostles, who were the earliest followers of Jesus and eyewitnesses to what Jesus said. He testifies that their witness was the true and authentic one. Their Gospels contain Jesus' teachings about Himself. What did Jesus teach His disciples concerning Himself? Here are just a handful of His claims to divinity.

- He allowed others to call Him the Christ (Matthew 16:15–20; 26:63–64).

- He said He could forgive sin (Matthew 9:2–6; Luke 7:47–48).

- He did not stop others from calling Him the Son of God (Matthew 14:33).

- He promised to rise from the dead (Matthew 20:18–19; 27:62–63).

- He said He would be the ultimate judge at the end of time (Matthew 25:31–46).

Would You Die for a Lie?

Those who saw *The Passion of the Christ,* the incredibly moving film directed by Mel Gibson, will recall the horrific torture that Jesus endured before His death. The cruelty was extreme, even to the Romans who were masters of extreme cruelty. Why would a "good" man endure such punishment? If Jesus did not believe Himself to be divine, why did He not confess His deception and avoid such agony?

Those who followed Jesus in life also followed Him in death. These, too, could have avoided needless suffering had they but declared that Jesus was just a man. But they did not. According to oral traditions passed down from the early church, here is how some of Jesus' disciples met their end:

- James the son of Zebedee was beheaded.
- Simon Peter was crucified in Rome. It is said that, at his request, he was crucified upside down, saying, "I am not worthy to die in the manner of Jesus."
- Paul was beheaded by Nero in A.D. 66.
- Stephen was stoned by a mob in A.D. 38.

These are but a few of the martyrs who did not deny Jesus' divinity. If Jesus' followers did not hold Him to be the Son of God, if that truly was a fourth-century invention, all these men died for no reason at all.

SUDDENLY DIVINE?

Let's return to *The Da Vinci Code*'s assertion that Jesus was not considered divine until the year A.D. 325, when Constantine, for political purposes, manipulated some bishops to "vote" Jesus divine. In addition to evidence from Paul and the writings of the early church, there are many more confirmations of the divinity of Jesus. All of these demonstrate that long before the Council of Nicaea, the leaders of the church considered Jesus divine. Here is what several of these leaders wrote (years approximate):

- Ignatius: "God Himself was manifested in human form" (A.D. 105).
- Clement: "It is fitting that you should think of Jesus Christ as of God" (A.D. 150).
- Justin Martyr: "The Father of the universe has a Son. And He ... is even God" (A.D. 160).
- Irenaeus: "He is God, for the name Emmanuel indicates this" (A.D. 180).
- Tertullian: "... Christ our God" (A.D. 200).
- Origen: "No one should be offended that the Savior is also God ..." (A.D. 225).
- Novatian: "... He is not only man, but God also ..." (A.D. 235).
- Cyprian: "Jesus Christ, our Lord and God" (A.D. 250).
- Methodius: "... He truly was and is ... with God, and being God ..." (A.D. 290).
- Lactantius: "We believe Him to be God" (A.D. 304).
- Arnobius: "Christ performed all those miracles ... the ... duty of Divinity" (A.D. 305).[3]

WHAT REALLY HAPPENED AT THE COUNCIL OF NICAEA?

Brown's character, Teabing, warms to the subject of the Nicaean Council while teaching Sophie about Jesus:

> "Jesus' establishment as the 'Son of God' was officially proposed and voted on by the Council of Nicaea."
>
> "Hold on. You're saying Jesus' divinity was the result of a *vote*?"
>
> "A relatively close vote at that," Teabing added (233).

Councils held to determine important doctrinal matters were not uncommon to the early Christians. We read in Acts 15 how the church leaders came together to decide how Gentiles were to be treated. Councils were important in order to maintain an orthodox faith and prevent the spread of false teaching.

One such false teaching was being spread by Arius in A.D. 318. Arius taught that Jesus was a created being, just like other humans, and not the "begotten Son of God." He was opposed by Alexander, the bishop of Alexandria, who declared Arius a heretic in a local council in A.D. 321. So Arius moved to Palestine and continued his teaching there. If he had kept his ideas to his own followers, there would not have been cause to call a council. But Arius began sending letters to area churches promoting the idea of Jesus as a created being. The debate grew over the next few years, finally gaining the attention of the emperor, Constantine.

The vote was 316 to 2. That can hardly be called a close vote.

THE NICENE CREED

We believe in one God,
the Father, the
Almighty,
maker of heaven and
earth,
of all that is, seen and
unseen.

We believe in one Lord,
Jesus Christ,
the only Son of God,
eternally begotten of
the Father,
God from God, Light
from Light,
true God from true
God,
begotten, not made,
of one Being with the
Father.
Through him all things
were made.
For us and for our
salvation
he came down from
heaven:
by the power of the
Holy Spirit
he became incarnate
from the Virgin Mary,
and was made man.

For our sake he was
crucified under
Pontius Pilate;

Constantine, who had consolidated his hold on the Roman Empire, sought unity in all regions. He knew that a division within the Christian church would be one more destabilizing force in the empire, so he moved to restore peace. Constantine called together more than 300 bishops from around the empire, primarily from the east. (This would have favored Arius's cause, as that is where his influence was greatest.) Bishops traveled thousands of miles to attend the conference held in Constantinople. Many came bearing wounds and scars from torture they had endured for their faith.

The Arians submitted their statement of doctrine that flatly denied the divinity of Christ. It was soundly rejected. The bishops, led by Athanasius, considered what was taught by the original church in the writings of the New Testament. These men wrote up an alternative creed, which became the blueprint for the Nicene Creed. In it Jesus was affirmed to be divine, the historic position of the church for the previous three hundred years.

The new creed was adopted. Only

two voted against. That can hardly be called a close vote. The church had suffered for three centuries under the tyranny of the Roman Empire. The Council of Nicaea came only fourteen years after the final persecution of Christians at the hands of Emperor Galerius. The bishops of the church would never have compromised what had cost their fellow Christians so much. They would have rather suffered another three centuries of oppression and persecution than deny their Lord.

Yet *The Da Vinci Code* makes this, one of the most sublime theological legacies of the ancient church, appear to be mere political propaganda. Even if Constantine's motives were not driven by his desire for correct doctrine, which no one knows, it doesn't matter. The evidence of history and the light of Scripture affirm the divinity of Christ. The apostles, the persecuted church, and the Nicene bishops did not revise history, they affirmed it. For them it certainly was not "the greatest story ever sold." Many paid for their faith with their own blood.

he suffered death and was buried.
On the third day he rose again
in accordance with the Scriptures;
he ascended into heaven
and is seated at the right hand of the Father.
He will come again in glory to judge the living and the dead, and his kingdom will have no end.

We believe in the Holy Spirit, the Lord, the giver of life,
who proceeds from the Father and the Son.
With the Father and the Son he is worshiped and glorified.
He has spoken through the Prophets.
We believe in one holy catholic and apostolic Church.
We acknowledge one baptism for the forgiveness of sins.
We look for the resurrection of the dead, and the life of the world to come.
AMEN.

If the code is left unchallenged when it denies the divinity of Jesus, another part of the Divine Arc is removed.

CHAPTER 5

Is it true that the church has rewritten history to present a one-sided account of the faith (233–235)?

Is it true that the church Dan Brown refers to is the true church?

Is it true that the church has suppressed knowledge about a marriage between Jesus and Mary Magdalene that, if known, would destroy Christianity (244, 249)?

Is it true that the church knows the whereabouts of the Holy Grail but has committed murder and employed "horrific" methods to keep this knowledge hidden (266)?

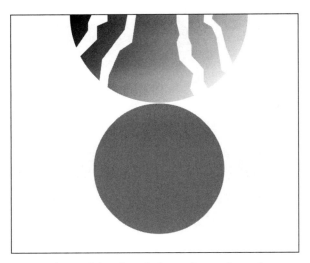

So, in place of the church Jesus formed, made
from those who confess His name and claim
Him as their Savior and Lord, *The Da Vinci Code*
proposes an up-to-date model made from all
kinds of faiths where neither the real Jesus nor
true salvation can be found. In so doing, another
part of the Sacred Arc is removed.

WHO IS REVISING HISTORY?

... the Church had a deceitful and violent history. Their brutal crusade to "reeducate" the pagan and feminine-worshipping religions spanned three centuries. (124)

"What gets me is how controlling the church has been all these years. And how gullible people are for going there week after week, being led around like a bunch of cattle with rings in their noses."

Carrie purposely did not add, "like you." She liked Evan and didn't want to push him away.

"Oh, so that's what you talk about at those book club meetings each week. How the church has a great secret it needs to hide, so it made up an elaborate lie, covered it in symbols and codes, and now uses the power of that secret to herd us around? Hmm, sounds to me like you're the ones being led like cattle."

"What do you mean?" Carrie shot Evan a glare that was meant to put him in his place, but he was looking up at a flock of geese returning from their winter migration.

"You know," said Evan, neck still craned skyward, "we really should try to be more like geese." Evan was a Philosophy major, heading for divinity school next semester. Yet Carrie had come to know that his "discourses" were more like personal reflections than lectures or (shudder!) sermons.

"Why geese?"

"Well," said Evan as they resumed walking, "for one thing, geese fly in a V formation in order to help each other fly farther without getting as tired. When a goose flaps its wings, it creates a draft for the goose right behind it. When a goose breaks formation, it finds out quickly that going it alone is a lot harder."

"It must be tough for the one out in front with no one to help with the drafting."

"Well, when the leader gets tired," continued Evan, "he falls back and someone else takes the point. All the honking you hear is the other geese offering encouragement to the one up front."

"You sure do know your fowl," said Carrie.

"And get this." Evan totally missed the sarcasm in Carrie's voice. He used his arms to imitate a goose gliding. "If one goose gets tired or injured and starts toward the ground, two other geese will drop out of formation and go with it to offer protection. Once the injured goose is healed, they join up with another flock until they catch up with theirs or reach their destination."

Carrie swung in front of Evan and, glaring up into his eyes, demanded, "All right. Stop right there. Tell me, when did you become an Ag major?"

Evan laughed and shook his head. "Honest, Carrie—I'm still in Philosophy. That is, if I didn't totally blow my exam this morning. I learned about geese from my pastor. He was telling how Christians need to act toward one another like geese."

"You mean you talk about the flying habits of geese at your church? I thought you just chanted, ate stale bread and drank watery wine, and listened to some misogynist rail about sexual immorality."

Evan stopped laughing and looked down at Carrie. "Let's sit down for a moment, okay?" The two found the last empty table at the crowded coffee bar. Evan ordered a tall coffee with cream, and

Carrie ordered a latté. "So your idea of church is some kind of weird religious ritual and an anti-culture speech?"

"Either that," she said between sips, "or a political rant against the Democrats. And someone reading from an outdated, man-made—and I do emphasize the word *man*—book that no halfway intelligent person would believe in the first place."

"Wow, Carrie," Evan said, throwing up his hands in mock surrender. "Don't mince words. Tell me how you really feel."

Carrie blushed and said quickly, "I'm sorry. I just really don't have good feelings toward any church right now. Especially not after what I've been reading in *The Da Vinci Code*. Did you know that the church has purposely suppressed evidence throughout the centuries that proves Jesus and Mary Magdalene were married and had a child? They've killed people just to keep this secret."

"And you learned this reading a novel?" Evan asked.

"Everything the author says is fact, even if it is fiction." As soon as she said that, Carrie realized how foolish it sounded. To his credit, Evan did not pounce on her *faux pas*.

"I'd like to talk with you about Brown's book and his view of the church. First, though, if I may be so bold, I'd like to invite you to come to my church with me sometime. I think you'll find it just a bit different than you picture."

Carrie snorted with disgust. "Me? Church? You wouldn't catch me dead in a church."

"Well, maybe another time then. All right, let's see what else Professor Langdon has been teaching you."

⟞⊷⟝

There are hidden documents that prove the Bible's account of Jesus' life is false. These documents, if found and revealed, would show Jesus as a mortal who never rose from the dead. They would prove that Jesus and Mary Magdalene were married and had children together. They could point to persons alive today who are descendants of Jesus and Mary. And it is these secret documents, according to *The Da Vinci Code*, that hold the true historical records—not the Bible and the writings of the church fathers.

Did Christians conspire to stage a "fable agreed upon"?

Is it *true* that the church has rewritten history to present a one-sided account of the faith (233–235)?

Is it *true* that the church Dan Brown refers to is the true church?

Is it *true* that the church has suppressed knowledge about a marriage between Jesus and Mary Magdalene that, if known, would destroy Christianity (244, 249)?

Is it *true that* the church knows the whereabouts of the Holy Grail but has committed murder and employed "horrific" methods to keep this knowledge hidden (266)?

DID THE CHURCH REWRITE HISTORY TO LOOK GOOD?

Leigh Teabing, the famous historian in *The Da Vinci Code*, gives us a lesson in the making of historical records:

> "[H]istory is always written by the winners.
> When two cultures clash, the loser is obliterated,
> and the winner writes the history books—books

which glorify their own cause and disparage the conquered foe. As Napoleon once said, 'What is history, but a fable agreed upon?'" (256).

Who are we to believe? Dan Brown, through his characters, discounts the Bible with one sweep of his pen. He says that winners write history, implying that since Christians were the winners in the power struggle during the time of Constantine, they were able to rewrite history to their advantage. They staged a "fable agreed upon." The fable? That Jesus was a divine being who, after dying, rose from the dead. This, according to Teabing and Langdon, is not provable, so it must be a falsehood written by "winners."

In order to accept this theory as presented in *The Da Vinci Code*, we must deal with facts that cannot be disputed. We will look in detail at the assembly of our Bible in the next chapter. But for now, consider this point: A number of scholars make an excellent case that the New Testament books were all written before A.D. 70. At that time, as we discussed earlier, Christians were a minority, persecuted by both fellow Jews and the Romans. They could not, in any way, be considered "winners" when these books were written. They were killed for maintaining their faith when a simple verbal rejection of Jesus would have saved them from a cruel death. These are the ones Brown considers "winners"?

The Biblical Account: Warts and All

If the writers of the Bible were trying to manipulate history in their favor, why would they include so many accounts of the failures of their "star players"? For instance, the Bible clearly records the accounts of

- Adam and Eve disobeying God and bringing death on us all (Genesis 3; Romans 5:12–14);
- Abraham/Abram (Genesis 12:10–20), Isaac (Genesis 26:7–11), and Jacob (Genesis 27) lying and deceiving others;
- Moses committing murder (Exodus 2:11–14) and giving in to bursts of anger (Numbers 20:10–12);
- David covering up his affair with a married woman by having her husband killed (2 Samuel 11);
- Solomon, the wisest man who ever lived (1 Kings 4:30), showing a profound lack of wisdom on several occasions (1 Kings 11);
- Peter being impetuous and frequently saying and doing very foolish things (Matthew 16:22–23; 17:1–5; 26:33–34, 69–74);
- The mother of James and John, two of Jesus' closest associates, showing selfishness in her ambitions for her sons (Matthew 20:20–28); and
- Paul and Barnabas getting into a feud, not resolving it, and parting company (Acts 15:36–41).

If the pages of the Bible had been tampered with or rewritten to make its cause look good, those stories would have been deleted. In their place would be stories of how these men and women were perfect in every way.

And More Warts

If Christians truly were the "winners" who could rewrite history in their favor, why did they include in the list of church leaders men and women who were less than perfect?

- Origen misinterpreted a biblical text and, as penance, castrated himself.

- Augustine, the most influential figure in nearly one thousand years of church history, had a mistress and fathered and abandoned a son in his pre-Christian life.

- Jerome, the first man who ever translated the entire Bible, had a very contentious personality.

- Peter Abelard, one of the greatest theologians of the Middle Ages, had an affair that resulted in an illegitimate son.

- Canon Fulbert, who was the pastor at the Cathedral of Notre Dame at that time, overreacted and had Peter Abelard castrated.

- Martin Luther sometimes became inebriated, during which times he said some unfortunate things.

- John Calvin was demanding and rigid in his thinking.

- John Wesley had a pathetic marriage.

- The Puritans in the New World mistreated Roger Williams and Anne Hutchinson.

- D. L. Moody and Charles Spurgeon battled with depression.

- Aimee Semple McPherson, the well-known woman preacher of the early 1900s, tarnished her reputation by disappearing for a time in what appears to have been a staged kidnapping.

The church doesn't have to rewrite history to hide anything. The church, as someone has said, "is not a museum of saints, but a laboratory for sinners." People frequently fail in their desire to emulate Christ, and writers of church history—the inspired writers of the Bible as well as past- and present-day writers—are known for exposing, rather than trying to cover up, any of the blemishes of the church's very long story. If *The Da Vinci Code*'s thesis is correct that the church rewrites history, then we would not know all the stories of the failures of those who were part of the long history of the church.

THE "NOMINAL" CHURCH

Brown uses the term "Church" (with a capital C) throughout *The Da Vinci Code* synonymously with "Rome." (See page 266 of *The Da Vinci Code* for an example.) For both terms he is referring to the Roman Catholic Church. Since he spends much time going back and forth in the history of the early church, we feel it is important to slow down and look more closely at the formation of the church. This will reveal many of the significant points that *The Da Vinci Code* fails to tell.

From A.D. 100 until around A.D. 300, Christians remained a minority. At first they were, for the most part, tolerated or ignored by the Roman government. But as their influence increased, so did the persecution. Roman emperor Nero ordered the beheading of Paul and the crucifixion of Peter in A.D. 64. But it was not until the second century that Christianity was officially outlawed. Persecution was sporadic until the third century when Roman officials, trying to calm an increasingly panicked public, began widespread persecution of Christians. The people blamed the numerous barbaric invasions on these believers who held to their claim that there is only one God, thus showing disrespect to the pagan Roman gods.

Constantine's declaration resulted in the compromise of authentic Christianity.

The persecutions reached a crescendo at the beginning of the fourth century under co-emperors Diocletian and Galerius, who removed all Christians from places of influence in the government and military, burned churches, and tortured and killed Christians in the public arenas. Yet, through all of these violent acts perpetrated against the church, believers in Christ continued to increase in numbers faster than they could be killed. Clearly, those who chose to be identified as Christians did so because of their firm belief in Jesus and His radical teachings. At that point in history, there was no rational reason to be known as a follower of the Christ. Again, these were not winners rewriting history.

Compromise, Not Conversion

In A.D. 312, Constantine was proclaimed emperor of the West. He credited the Christian God with helping him to win the military battles that led to this proclamation. In A.D. 313, he met with the emperor of the East in Milan, where they both declared tolerance toward all religions, especially Christianity. While on the surface this event would seem to be a major victory for the faith, it was almost its undoing.

Constantine set out to form a union between the Christian church and the Roman Empire. He gave land and money to the churches to rebuild what previous emperors had destroyed. The church began to depend on the Roman government for money not only to finance its buildings, but also to pay its leaders.

By A.D. 380, Christianity was the officially established religion of the entire Roman Empire. This declaration resulted, not in authentic conversion by which people willingly and knowingly embraced Christianity, but in a redefinition of what it meant to be a Christian, thus compromising authentic Christianity. Thousands simply declared themselves (or were forced to declare themselves) to be Christian, with no understanding of what that declaration meant. Brown's character Robert Langdon has it wrong. Rather than Christianity crushing paganism, the paganistic influence within the church caused great confusion among the believers.

This huge influx of pagans, now calling themselves Christians, created what we are calling the "nominal" ("in name only") church. The church that *The Da Vinci Code* generally presents is this nominal church, made up of people who *called* themselves "Christian" but who had no idea what the term meant.

THE "REAL" CHURCH

True believers were aghast at what they saw happening. This was a group of people—many of whom still bore scars from torture endured at the hands of the Romans—who believed in the living Christ enough that they were willing to suffer and die. These were men and women who, though they loved their pagan neighbors and wanted to see them converted, had no desire to embrace their gods. We will call this group the "real" church.

The real church was begun by Christ. It is first mentioned by Jesus in Matthew 16:18 in a discussion with Peter. But the most profound description of the church occurs in the second chapter of the book of Acts (2:42–47) in the New Testament—on the day that the church actually began. The real church consists of those who authentically embrace Christ as one who forgives their sins and who is to be Lord, directing their lives.

What Is a "Christian"?

If we raise the question regarding what a church is, that raises the question of what a "Christian" really is. Some people say, "I am a Christian." What they really mean by that is that they are not a Muslim, or a Jew, or a Buddhist, or a Hindu. But that does not make them a Christian. You are not a Christian simply because you are not a part of other religions. You are a Christian only to the extent that you are a follower of Christ as Savior and Lord. Simply saying you are a Christian doesn't make you a Christian. Simply saying you are part of the real church doesn't make you part of the real church.

THE PRIORY HOAX

The Priory of Sion, according to *The Da Vinci Code,* is one of the oldest secret societies still in existence. It is the Priory that has been charged with guarding the secret of the true Holy Grail, starting in 1099 when the Knights Templar discovered long-lost documents beneath the ruins of Solomon's Temple. Leonardo da Vinci was Grand Master of this society, says Robert Langdon, from 1510 to 1519. The only problem is this: It is all a hoax.

Brown relies on a 1982 publication, *Holy Blood, Holy Grail,* for his information on the Priory of Sion. The authors of *Holy Blood, Holy Grail* relied on documents provided them by Pierre Plantard, an anti-Semitic Frenchman who spent time in jail for fraud in 1953. Plantard and three other men started a small social club in 1954 called the Priory of Sion, taking the name from a nearby mountain. Their club's "cause" was the call for more low-cost housing in France. The club dissolved in 1957, but Plantard held on to the name.

Throughout the 1960s and the 1970s, Plantard created a series of documents "proving" the existence of a bloodline descending from Mary Magdalene, through the kings of France, down to the

Several years ago I (Jim) was flying home to San Diego. Seated next to me was an incredibly muscular young man. He was so phenomenally brawny that I finally decided to ask him what he did to get so big. I found out that he was preparing for the Olympics, in the hammer throw competition. I asked him why he was flying to San Diego. He explained to me that he was coming to the Olympic Training Center that is located in Chula Vista. When we landed, I got off the plane before he did, found my suitcases at the baggage claim, and went outside to meet my ride.

As I waited at the curb, I glanced to my left and saw a van from the Olympic Training Center. Inside it sat three enormously muscular men, all in their twenties. They were obviously a part of the hammer throw competition and were there to meet their friend who had been seated beside me on the plane. Since I knew his name, I decided to play a practical joke. I walked up to those three monstrous men and said, "Are you looking for Joe Smith?" (That isn't his real name.) They said, "Yes." I said, "I'm him. I'm here. I'm so glad to meet you!" I began to shake their hands excitedly as though I was one of the members of their team.

It took only a fraction of a second for it to register on them what was happening. The look on their faces was first one of shock, then disappointment; then a nanosecond later, it changed to a "wait a minute" kind of look. They immediately knew this was a practical joke. They said, "No you're not—surely you're not—you can't be him!"

Putting them on the spot, I quickly responded, "Why do you say that? What makes you think I'm not him?" None of them wanted to say the obvious: "Because you don't have

present day to include (surprise!) Pierre Plantard. He began using the name Plantard de Saint-Clair, saying the Saint-Clairs were direct descendants of the line of Jesus and Mary.

In 1993, Plantard's name came up in light of a political scandal involving a close friend of then French president François Mitterand. Plantard had, in one of his documented lists of the Priory of Sion, listed Roger-Patrice Pelat as a Grand Master. When called before the court to testify, Plantard, under oath, admitted he had made up the whole Priory scheme. The court ordered a search of Plantard's house, which revealed further documents that proclaimed Plantard to be the true king of France. The judge gave Plantard a stern warning and dismissed him as a harmless crank.[1]

If that judge had known the far-reaching impact of Plantard's fraud, he might have taken stronger action to censure the materials that Plantard had generated. While there are numerous books and articles revealing Plantard's hoax for what it is, they do not prove as exciting as a conspiracy thriller. Thus, millions of readers are being reintroduced to Plantard's fantasies through the writings of Dan Brown in the fictional *The Da Vinci Code*.

the muscular physique to be able to do what we do. If *you* are on our team, we will most assuredly lose our chance to go to the Olympics." No one said that. But I could tell they were all thinking it.

There are people who *say* they are a part of the church, but when you spend a little bit of time with them you find out quickly they do not embrace Jesus Christ as Lord and Savior, and they do not follow the teachings of the Bible. Therefore, just *saying* you're part of the church does not make you part of the church any more than my saying I was on the Olympic Hammer Throw Team made me an athlete.

There is much about the church of the Middle Ages that is inexcusable.

Would the Real Church Please Stand Up?

The Da Vinci Code often selects some of the things that people did in the name of the church that are not representative of the true church. By focusing on these activities, it condemns all of Christianity. Is *The Da Vinci Code* correct that "the Church" abused people? The answer is both yes and no. It depends on which church is being referred to. The nominal church does not look to Christ as being fully sufficient for salvation, nor is it concerned with adherence to the Bible. Thus it has, most certainly, abused many. And it consistently violates the Bible. An obvious example is the Roman Catholic Inquisition in the Middle Ages, in which people were tortured and killed if they deviated from the dogma and structure of the church at that time.

The point is this: There is much about the church of the Middle Ages that is inexcusable. No one can defend it. No one should. At the same time, the *true* church of the time was comprised of many spectacular Christians who reflected Jesus Christ powerfully and who were also part of the Roman Catholic Church. Thus when Brown says "the Church," he sloppily includes the true church of the Middle Ages. This might make an engaging novel. But it is a distortion of history.

JESUS AND MARY MAGDALENE

The next question we need to answer deals with the relationship between Jesus and Mary Magdalene. Brown wants us to believe that the church has, throughout history, conducted a "smear campaign" to malign the character of Mary Magdalene. It is, according to Brown, part of the church's overall effort to remove the "goddess" from our worship. He shows this through a bizarre speculation into da Vinci's *Last Supper* fresco, as well as wrong teachings about the church's portrayal of Mary Magdalene.

Langdon and Teabing are teaching Sophie Neveu about the Holy Grail as they examine a reproduction of da Vinci's *Last Supper* in a book:

> Sophie scanned the work eagerly. "Does this fresco tell us *what* the Grail really is?"
>
> "Not *what* it is," Teabing whispered. "But rather *who* it is. The Holy Grail is not a thing. It is, in fact, a ... *person*" (236).

Langdon and Teabing go on to explain to Sophie how da Vinci, in his famous fresco, allegedly depicted Mary Magdalene as one of the disciples. From this, and other sources they quote, they deduce that Mary was Jesus' companion ("the word *companion*, in those days, literally meant *spouse*," says Teabing [246]) and the two had a child together. Thus, from this hypothesis it is presented that Mary herself is the Holy Grail, the recipient of the seed of Jesus. From this scenario, Brown weaves his code—the return of goddess worship into our culture.

Earlier, Professor Langdon tellingly contemplates: "A career hazard of symbologists was a tendency to extract hidden meaning from situations that had none," (171–172). Unintentionally, this statement aptly describes the fantasies of *The Da Vinci Code* with regard to Mary Magdalene. Teabing explains to Sophia Neveu, "The Church needed to defame Mary Magdalene in order to cover up her dangerous secret— her role as the Holy Grail." (244). Thus, the thinking follows, the church engineered a smear campaign to portray her as a prostitute. Langdon was right that *"[e]veryone loves a conspiracy"* (169). Brown, using discredited sources (see sidebar), tells a conspiracy tale like no other. Not only was Mary Magdalene Jesus' companion, but their relationship produced a child. And that bloodline lives today. Brown draws much of this conjecture from *Holy Blood, Holy Grail*. The authors of this 1982 non-fiction book go even further in their depiction of Mary as the Grail:

There is no credible record that Jesus was married.

> If our hypothesis is correct, the Holy Grail would have been at least two things simultaneously. On the one hand, it would have been Jesus' bloodline and descendants—the "Sang Raal," the "Real" or "Royal" blood of which the Templars, created by the Prieuré de Sion, were appointed guardians. At the same time the Holy Grail would have been, quite literally, the receptacle or vessel that received and contained Jesus' blood. In other words it would have been the womb of the Magdalen—and by extension, the Magdalen herself.[2]

According to Brown's Leigh Teabing, "the marriage of Jesus and Mary Magdalene is part of the historical record" (245).

There is no credible historical record that Jesus was married. None. We will not even enter the debate as to whether Jesus was married or not. This is simply, from a biblical and historical perspective, a non-issue, despite even the patently false supposition that Jews in Jesus' time were somehow forbidden to remain unmarried (245).

Was Mary Magdalene a Prostitute?

There is no evidence that the early church tried to tarnish Mary Magdalene's reputation by making her out to be a prostitute. Any reference to her as a prostitute does not come from the Bible. Here is what we do know of Mary from the biblical record:

- Seven demons were cast out of her by Jesus (Luke 8:2);
- She witnessed the horror of the crucifixion (Matthew 27:32–56);

- She was present at the burial of Jesus (Matthew 27:57–61);

- She, along with two other women, went to anoint the body of Jesus (Mark 16:1);

- She was the first person to see Jesus in His resurrected body (John 20:10–18).

Some have surmised that since her name and story appear immediately following the account of a prostitute, the two are one and the same woman (see Luke 7:36 through 8:2). But there is no biblical support for this conclusion. (Most historians agree that the reference to Mary Magdalene as a prostitute was started in the sixth century by Pope Gregory I.) Still others have conjectured that she is the anonymous woman caught in adultery. There is no evidence to support that assumption, either. Some have guessed that she might have been a prostitute simply because she came from Magdala, which was often associated with prostitution. Once again, the Bible says no such thing. Any association of Mary of Magdala with either of the above-mentioned anonymous women would have been merely a result of conjecture—or very careless scholarship—probably dating to the Middle Ages, as opposed to a smear campaign.

We do know that Mary Magdalene was a follower of Christ. We also know that Jesus ministered to her, as He did to hundreds—perhaps thousands—of men and women. And—most important—we know that she was the first person ever to report that Jesus was risen from the dead.

Instead of questioning her reputation, the Bible assigns to her one of the highest honors of all time: announcing of the single most important event in history, the resurrection.

For that matter, the Bible does record that many so-called people of disrepute did believe and follow after Jesus. Indeed, the apostle Matthew himself was called from the ranks of "sinners," being a traitorous tax collector, arguably lower in Jewish social standing than a prostitute (Matthew 9:9–12). So even if Mary Magdalene could have

Any reference to Mary Magdalene as a prostitute does not come from the Bible.

been proven a prostitute, how could there have been any "smearing" on the part of biblical Christians? To the frustration of the "righteous" religious leaders of the time, Jesus' way was to associate with and bring into his fold those who were considered outcasts and socially unacceptable.

HAS THE CHURCH HIDDEN THE HOLY GRAIL?

On the surface, *The Da Vinci Code* is about the search for the hiding place of the Holy Grail. At its core, there is a much greater message—a code we are attempting to crack. But let us look now to this quest for the Holy Grail. Is the church really suppressing knowledge of such an item through means that include extortion and murder?

Most of us, if we were familiar with the Holy Grail at all

before *The Da Vinci Code*, probably associated it with the Monty Python or Indiana Jones movies in which the heroes were on a Grail quest. Some will associate it with Arthurian legends. But there are few who know its origins.

The Grail lore came about in the latter part of the twelfth and early part of the thirteenth centuries. It varied from a simple dish a hermit saw in a vision to fantastic tales of miracles done by a cup or dish. One story holds that Joseph of Arimathea took the Grail with him when he was imprisoned. Food miraculously appeared each day in the Grail for the next forty-two years. Other stories promote similar magical qualities. The stories that tell of the quest for the Grail became intertwined with legends of King Arthur, but they all disappeared after the thirteenth century, later reappearing in the nineteenth century in a poem by Alfred Lord Tennyson (*Idylls of the King*) and music by Richard Wagner. And, of course, the latest manifestations have been in several twentieth-century films.

The Roman Catholic Church did not originate the idea of the Grail, nor does it promote the Grail as a sacred relic. From the *Catholic Encyclopedia*:

> Excepting Helanindus [a historian writing in the
> thirteenth century], clerical writers do not mention
> the Grail, and the Church ignored the legend com-
> pletely. After all, the legend contained the elements
> of which the Church could not approve. Its sources
> are in apocryphal, not in canonical, scripture, and
> the claims of sanctity made for the Grail were
> refuted by their very extravagance. As we have

seen, the whole tradition concerning the Grail is of late origin and on many points at variance with historical truth. [3]

Yet Langdon claims, "The Grail is literally the ancient symbol for womanhood, and the *Holy* Grail represents the sacred feminine and the goddess, which of course has now been lost, virtually eliminated by the Church" (238).

In Brown's code, the church is actively suppressing the identity of the Grail. This could not be further from the truth. The hard reality is, the Grail remains—as it has always been—an inconsequential legend to Christians of the real church: at best a novelty, but to most an aberration.

YES, WE BELIEVE THERE IS A HOLY GRAIL

Is there a real Holy Grail? No, there is no physical Grail. There is not a magic dish like the one mentioned in the medieval stories, nor is there the simple, wooden cup Indiana Jones chooses in *The Last Crusade*. And we can say for certain that the Holy Grail is not, as Brown would have you believe, Mary Magdalene or her offspring.

But there is a spiritual sense in which the Holy Grail might be said to be real.

The authors of *Holy Blood, Holy Grail* unknowingly hit on a truth in the legend of the Grail. They write that the Grail is "the receptacle or vessel that received and contained Jesus' blood." They are absolutely correct, but they are looking for this vessel in all the wrong places. In fact, this Grail can be seen clearly in Leonardo da Vinci's fresco,

Yes, the Grail can be seen clearly in da Vinci's fresco, The Last Supper.

The Last Supper. Listen to Jesus' words during that meal:

While they were eating, Jesus took a loaf of bread, and after blessing it he broke it, gave it to the disciples, and said, "Take, eat; this is my body." Then he took a cup, and after giving thanks he gave it to them, saying, "Drink from it, all of you; for this is my blood of the covenant, which is poured out for many for the forgiveness of sins" (Matthew 26:26–28 NRSV).

The Holy Grail *is* the receptacle of Jesus' blood, shed on the cross by a sinless Man to provide forgiveness for sinful men and women. But this Holy Grail is not a limited biological or ethnic reality (the physical seed of Jesus, as Brown contends); rather, it's a multi-ethnic, global, spiritual fellowship made up of all kinds of forgiven sinners. In other words, those who receive forgiveness through the blood of Jesus are the Holy Grail. The real church, made up of forgiven sinners from every gender, race, nation, and socioeconomic group, is the spiritual Holy Grail.

BROWN'S IDEAL CHURCH

What kind of church does Brown advocate? He tipped his hand in the book he wrote just prior to *The Da Vinci Code*.

Brown introduced Robert Langdon in *Angels and Demons*, another exciting, fast-paced novel with a religious theme underneath the action. In this book, Langdon is working side by side with Vittoria Vetra to prevent a disaster in the Vatican. During one of their conversations, the topic turns to faith. Vittoria tells Langdon:

> Faith is universal. Our specific methods for under-standing it are arbitrary. Some of us pray to Jesus, some of us go to Mecca, some of us study sub-atomic particles. In the end we are all just search-ing for truth, that which is greater than ourselves.[4]

Brown undermines the biblical picture of the church and substitutes his own vision in its place. Contrast Jesus' church (one in which sinners are saved through the blood sacrifice of God-become-man) with Brown's vision of the ideal church: one in which everyone is doing what feels good at the time; one in which there is acceptance of all beliefs without distinc-tion. It is another part of his code.

So, in place of the church Jesus formed, made from those who confess His name and claim Him as their Savior and Lord, The Da Vinci Code *proposes an up-to-date model made from all kinds of faiths where neither the real Jesus nor true salvation can be found. In so doing, another part of the Sacred Arc is removed.*

⟫◆⟪

CHAPTER 6

Is it true that "The Bible is a product of man, ... Not of God" (241)?

Is it true that "the New Testament is false testimony" (342)?

Is it true that "the modern Bible was compiled and edited by men who possessed a political agenda ... to solidify their own power base" (234)?

Is it true that the chief player in this political move was Constantine, who supposedly "commissioned and financed a new Bible, which omitted those gospels that spoke of Christ's *human* traits and embellished those gospels that made Him godlike" (234)?

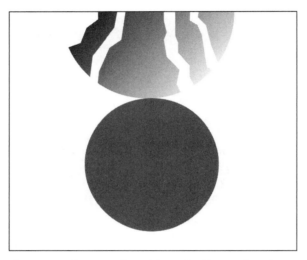

One more element, the Bible as God's Word and
unique message of salvation, is erased from the Arc.

DON'T SHOOT THE CANON

"Constantine commissioned and financed a new Bible, which omitted those gospels that spoke of Christ's human traits and embellished those gospels that made Him godlike. The earlier gospels were outlawed, gathered up, and burned" (234).

Carrie looked forward to Tuesday nights even more than the weekend; discussing *The Da Vinci Code* with her fellow students was invigorating. But tonight she had another reason to be excited as eight o'clock drew near. Evan had agreed to come to the readers' club with her. She tried to convince herself this was not a date, that she would never go out with a practicing Christian, but that didn't stop her heart from pounding every time she thought of him.

Right at eight o'clock, Evan ducked his six-foot-six frame through the door and sat down next to Carrie.

"Hope I'm not late," he said, slightly out of breath. "Had to run a quick errand."

"No, we haven't started yet—you're fine." Carrie noticed Evan had brought his backpack, and it seemed to be jammed full of books.

In another few minutes, Jen came striding into the room, accompanied by a woman Carrie had seen on campus before.

"Okay, let's get going," said Jen. Carrie knew Jen loved to be in charge. "We have a guest with us tonight. Dr. Susan Campbell teaches in the university and has graciously accepted my invitation to talk with us about tonight's subject. Dr. Campbell is an expert on the Bible, both the Bible we have been told for centuries is the one, true Bible, and the books that should have been included but were not. This is discussed in chapter 55 of *The Da Vinci Code*. Dr. Campbell?"

Jen took a seat, not in the front but in the semicircle next to Carrie. Dr. Campbell sat in the leader's chair.

"I am so glad you ladies—and gentleman" (here Dr. Campbell nodded to Evan; Jay hadn't shown up this evening) "are discussing this fascinating and important book." She held up a copy of *The Da Vinci Code*. "It reads like a novel, but it could almost be a textbook. I assume you all have read the book—at least through chapter 55?" Heads nodded in acknowledgment. Dr. Campbell continued. "Dan Brown has written what I have been speaking about for many years. I was raised in a conservative church and read the Bible often as I was growing up. It was a great source of comfort and encouragement, prodding me to do good deeds for others.

"But once I started studying how this Book came together—I did my undergraduate work at Smith and received my Ph.D. from Harvard—I realized how false and contrived it really is. What we have been taught in Sunday school about the Bible is as far from the truth as the notion that the moon is made of cheese."

Carrie leaned forward in her chair. She was so glad to have this eminent scholar speak on this topic. The whole subject of the biblical "canon" was confusing to her, at least when she read about it in *The Da Vinci Code*. She was sure Dr. Campbell could explain it in a way she would understand.

The guest speaker was now standing at a white board that had been set up, writing dates from top to bottom. She explained the political situation in the fourth century that greeted Constantine when he assumed the role of emperor. Names like Marcion, Arius, and Eusebius were written next to certain dates. "It all came to a

This drawing shows the traditional identifications of the twelve disciples as they are portrayed in da Vinci's painting. All twelve are listed in several places in the New Testament, including Matthew 10:2-4: "These are the names of the twelve apostles: first, ① Simon (who is called Peter) and his

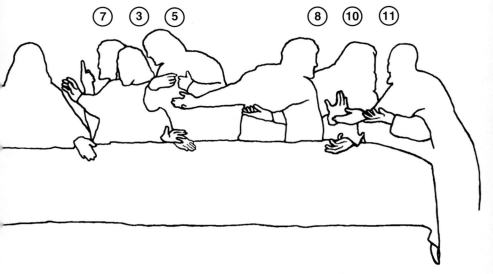

brother ② Andrew; ③ James son of Zebedee, and his brother
④ John; ⑤ Philip and ⑥ Bartholomew; ⑦ Thomas and ⑧ Matthew
the tax collector; ⑨ James son of Alphaeus, and ⑩ Thaddaeus;
⑪ Simon the Zealot and ⑫ Judas Iscariot, who betrayed him" (NIV).

The Last Supper fresco is on the northern wall of the refectory in the Convent of Santa Maria delle Grazie in Milan, Italy. Leonardo da Vinci used a mixture of egg tempera on dry plaster, giving his work a more varied palette but causing it to be less durable. The plaster began flaking off the wall almost as soon as da Vinci completed the fresco in the late 1490s.

Starting in 1726, there have been seven restorations of *The Last Supper*, with the most recent completed in 1999. The painting is now protected with a specialized air filtration system, and visitors are limited to groups of 25 staying no longer than 15 minutes.

boil," said Dr. Campbell, "at a council in the town of Nicaea. It was here that Constantine and a group of bishops—the types who would feel comfortable in fundamental churches today—made up what is known as the biblical canon. But what is even more important than the books they chose is the material they did not choose."

She erased the board and began listing titles under the heading Gnostic Gospels.

"These are all books that Constantine and the fundamentalist bishops threw out. Why? Because they challenged the power these men were trying to gather for themselves. The Gnostic Gospels tell quite a different story from what you would read in the accepted Bible. These are books that show you how you have the power within to make a new you. To be, in effect, truly born again."

To Carrie's surprise, Evan stood up, holding his backpack in his left hand. What was he doing? "Dr. Campbell," he started, "could I say something?" He reached into his bag and pulled out a paperback copy of the Bible.

"Uh-oh," the professor groaned. "Someone let a fundamentalist into the room." Everyone laughed, and someone even murmured something about kicking him out. Carrie kept quiet.

"Okay, I'll leave," he said. Carrie was surprised to see that he still smiled. "But I'd like to give you some copies of the Bible for your studies." He opened the bag and pulled out a handful, then another, of paperback Bibles and laid them out on a table near the door. "I think you'll be amazed to discover the truth in it. Dr. Campbell says that you have the power within you to make a new you; but if you understand how impossible that is, open this Book to find the One who will do it for you." He smiled at Carrie and left.

After a few moments of awkward silence, the group resumed their discussion. Dr. Campbell remarked that while she was sure the young man who just left had good intentions, fundamentalists were the greatest danger to truth and knowledge. She handed out a bibliography with a listing of books she claimed would show a much truer picture of the historical Jesus than the traditional Bible. "No real scholar gives the Bible much credence these days," she said. "You will, I'm sure, see a more realistic portrait of Jesus, and find yourself more clearly, in a book like the Gospel of Thomas."

Jen then concluded the meeting by saying they would meet next week in her dorm room. "We have a surprise for you," she said. "Come with an open mind and an open heart. I think you'll leave feeling more alive than ever before."

As Carrie left she noticed no one picked up any of the Bibles. She put her purse down on the table and slipped on her jacket. Then, careful that no one would see her, she picked up one of the Bibles and, shielding it with her purse, hurried out the door.

———

The Bible is the best-selling book in the history of publishing. It has been translated into thousands of languages and is read by millions every day. Yet if what *The Da Vinci Code* says about the origins of this book are true ("The Bible is a product of man, my dear. Not of God" [231]), then the Bible is not the inspired Word that reveals the Creator to creation, but a cruel hoax that has deceived followers for thousands of years.

Is it true that "The Bible is a product of man, ... Not of God" (231)?

Is it true that "the New Testament is false testimony" (345)?

Is it true that "the modern Bible was compiled and edited by men who possessed a political agenda ... to solidify their own power base" (234)?

Is it true that the chief player in this political move was

Constantine, who supposedly "commissioned and financed a new Bible, which omitted those gospels that spoke of Christ's *human* traits and embellished those gospels that made Him godlike" (234)?

(Peter): My mind goes back some thirty years to an event forever etched in my memory. I entered the smoke-filled seminar room with apprehension. At the oblong table sat thirty professors and graduate students, many cleaning pipes or lighting them, all frighteningly intense academics. I did not know it, but I was in a roomful of Robert Langdons. For me, a young, pipeless Christian "fundamentalist," this was a scary situation, and it got worse. The presiding professor looked around the room, and his eyes fell on me. I froze. "Mr. Jones, would you please begin translating the Qumran Hebrew text I have just circulated?"

I did not know it, but I was in a roomful of Robert Langdons.

That was my first experience in a Harvard graduate seminar. I soon learned that many of these brilliant scholars were committed to undermining the faith I held dear. Though not every liberal-minded scholar would use Teabing's lingo, current opinion (at least among the more radical) holds that the Bible is the product of men with a political agenda. For me, Christianity without the Bible was unthinkable. For two thousand years people had considered the "good book" the unique source of Christianity. But this was the last thing many of my professors believed.

The agenda of liberal religious scholarship used to be

hidden away in dry, dusty tomes on university library shelves. Now it has burst into view in an attractive novel and soon in an action-packed movie. Now everyone who has read *The Da Vinci Code* has learned what I learned in the academic world thirty-some years ago. Now many are asking, *Is the Bible a product of political conspiracy?* The question demands a serious response.

Is the Bible fact or is it fiction?

WHAT IS A "CANON" AND WHY DOES IT MATTER?

Canon is not an enormous gun from antiquity found in museums. That is *cannon* with a double N. Canon with one N refers to the recognized list of authentic books that make up the Bible—both Old and New Testaments. *The Da Vinci Code* suggests that this list was created in the fourth century.

Marcion: The Mouse That Roared

We've all heard about modern church leaders denying major doctrines of the Christian faith that they are required to uphold. Marcion (A.D. 90–160) from Pontus, in what is now Turkey, was one of those "modern" church leaders. Excommunicated for adultery by his bishop (his own father), Marcion took his revenge on the ultimate Father.

Was Marcion doing what Robert Langdon in *The Da Vinci Code* told his Harvard undergraduates to do: enjoy illicit sex and invent a spirituality to go with it? If he was, Marcion took the challenge very seriously. He got rid of marriage and declared the Old Testament—its laws and its God—unacceptable and out of date. Sound familiar? The same voices can be heard in scholarship today. As a great sage once wrote, there really isn't anything new under the sun (Ecclesiastes 1:9).

Marcion went to Rome in A.D. 144 and set up an alternative community. There he was excommunicated for doctrinal heresy, since he denied the essentials of the Christian faith and created his own Bible!

Marcion's Bible consisted of the Gospel of Luke and ten of Paul's letters, all "cleansed" of Old Testament influences. Marcion even acknowledged that the books he rejected or modified were accepted and honored by the church and written by the original apostles. He simply believed that he was right and they were wrong.

The church fathers were not gentle with Marcion. Tertullian (A.D. 160–255), not without a touch of humor, called him "the Pontic mouse who nibbled away the Gospels … abolished marriage … and tore God almighty to bits with [his] blasphemies."[1] Polycarp (A.D. 69–155), who knew the apostle John personally, upon meeting Marcion, called him "the first-born of Satan."[2]

One retired Episcopal bishop calls for the elimination of the God of the Bible.

Ironically, one hundred fifty years before Constantine, Marcion himself had already raised the issue of the Canon. Indeed, he confirms that a canon very close to our New Testament was already circulating in the latter part of the second century. Most scholars concur that the New Testament was essentially formed in the late second century as a reaction to the canon of Marcion. For the vast majority of scholars of all religious persuasions, *The Da Vinci Code*'s fourth-century date is therefore out of the question.

But even this second-century date may not go back far enough. To think that the debate with Marcion around A.D. 140 was the first time church leaders had thought about the Canon defies belief. A recognized Bible scholar calls this idea "pure speculation."[3] Marcion carved away much of what was already canonical in the church, "nibbling" away (as Tertullian put it) at what was already there. Marcion did not create the Canon. He gets a footnote in its history only because of his sheer audacity in trying to destroy it. The mouse's roar echoes today what he doubtless never intended: that *The Da Vinci Code*'s allegations of a Nicene canon conspiracy behind the Bible is pulp fiction.

Canon in the Bible

Canon is a very *biblical* idea. *Bible* means "book," and the Christian faith is established in books and written documents. Here is the antithesis to Brown's version of the Bible's history—the first generations of the Christian movement stated loudly and clearly the *biblical* nature of their faith. They believed in a written canon, beginning with the Old Testament; and they believed the Canon to be uniquely inspired by God himself.

It is telling that *The Da Vinci Code* critiques early Christianity with barely a mention of the Old Testament. The writers of the New Testament hailed the Old as the uniquely and divinely inspired written authority for everything they held dear. Jesus and the apostles held to the Canon of the Old Testament that Marcion would later reject. Jesus said

His life's mission was to fulfill the Old Testament: "Do not think that I have come to abolish the Law or the Prophets [he is referring to Old Testament Scripture] ... but to fulfill them" (Matthew 5:17).

The first day of church history is marked by a public sermon explaining the Old Testament Scripture (Acts 2). Peter, who gave that sermon as the leading apostle and appointed by Jesus, saw the Old Testament as inspired by the Spirit of God and as the confirming word for everything he taught (2 Peter 1:19–21). Paul, at the command of the Risen Christ, took the original Christian message to the pagan world and established the Old Testament "God-breathed" Scripture as the authoritative source of the church's entire teaching about the meaning of Jesus (2 Timothy 3:16–17). The Old Testament was received as a special, inspired "canonical" word from God Himself. Luke, who wrote the book of Acts, commended the people who lived in a town called Berea because they scrupulously examined the Old Testament to see if Paul's message could be believed (Acts 17:11).

The New Testament fulfills these previous canonical Scriptures. The inspired Old Testament texts are cited everywhere in New Testament writings to show that the New fulfills the Old. Jesus taught His disciples that the whole Old Testament was about Him (Luke 24:27). Paul agreed: Christ is the end goal or fulfillment, the final installment, of the Old Testament (Romans 10:4). Thus, the New Testament writers themselves claimed to be specially appointed by Christ to produce firsthand, God-inspired, written testimony to His astonishing life, death, and resurrection as the final chapter of the Canon.

Though Jesus did not write anything, He made sure there would be people, trained by Him, who would bring His message to the world. To write his Gospel, Luke indicates that firsthand eyewitnesses handed down their accounts directly to him (Luke 1:2); the apostle Peter claimed to be one of those "eyewitnesses" (2 Peter 1:16); the apostle John claimed to have "heard, seen, and touched" Jesus (1 John 1:1); and Paul claimed to have been the last to see the Risen Lord (1 Corinthians 15:8).

The apostle Peter, right from the outset of his first letter, flatly declared that Old Testament prophets foretold in their writings of Jesus' "sufferings" and "glories," and this foretelling happened centuries before Jesus ever appeared in the flesh on earth. Even though the prophets of old probably didn't fully fathom what they were writing (though they tried "to find out the time and circumstances"), they nevertheless faithfully communicated according to how they were inspired by the Holy Spirit, whom the apostle specified was sent by "Christ's Spirit" (1 Peter 1:11–12).

It's important to understand that all biblical references to "prophets" and "prophesying" first and foremost mean God was speaking through those humans, less than that they were foretelling the future. In fact, many writings by prophets don't even foretell; rather, they *forth*-tell from God. In Peter's second letter, he reaffirmed that "prophecy never had its origin in the will of man, but men spoke from God as they were carried along by the Holy Spirit" (2 Peter 1:21).

CHRIST'S ROCK AND THE APOSTLES' ROLE

I (Peter) understand what it means to be an eyewitness.

You've heard a lot about the famous John Lennon, but I shared a desk with him for five years. He and I used to slip away unnoticed from Quarrybank High School during school hours to buy fish and chips on Penny Lane. Once we threw textbooks out the second-story window of the school, and I "planted" the school gardener in the beautiful hole he had just dug and was leaning over. We also played a lot of music together. I might have become a Beatle, had my parents allowed me to go to clubs. (No regrets, by the way.)

I really did know John Lennon. We shared a desk for five years.

I remember how John and I were blown away as teenagers the first time we heard "Rock Around the Clock" by Bill Haley and the Comets. Rock and roll changed our lives, though John's more than mine. I have moved on to a variant of this theme—I wrote a Ph.D. dissertation on Christ's "rock" and the apostles' "role."[4]

I really did know John Lennon. I was an eyewitness.

The Bible is full of eyewitness testimony, confirming God's written prophecy. This is the rock on which Christ promised to build His church (Matthew 16:18). Jesus said of the apostles who lived with Him, watched Him, heard Him, and touched Him: "He who listens to you listens to me" (Luke 10:16). In other words, they were appointed as His mouthpiece. By the way, the "rock" is not left undefined. It

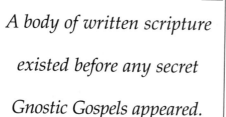

A body of written scripture existed before any secret Gnostic Gospels appeared.

was Peter who bore testimony to Jesus, the divine Son (Matthew 16:16). When Peter blurted out that Jesus is the Christ, Jesus told him it was His "Father in heaven" who revealed it to him (v. 17). A clearer definition of divine revelation will not be found, and it came from the mouth of Jesus Himself. This is the *role* the apostles would play.

Jesus also said that whatever the apostles allowed or disallowed on earth would be allowed or disallowed in heaven (Matthew 16:19). The apostles were given the keys of authority in the kingdom of heaven. This doesn't mean that Peter stands at the "pearly gates," the way so many jokes have it, holding a great big golden key. The "key" given to the apostles was the task of revealing the Gospel as the way of salvation. Paul used a different but parallel image. He said that the apostles were the foundation of the church (Ephesians 2:20). There is no other foundation than this solid rock (1 Corinthians 3:11). The apostles and prophets formed the foundation by speaking and teaching but also by writing and exhorting coming generations to "guard what has been entrusted" (1 Timothy 6:20; see also 2 Timothy 1:12–14).

This witness of Paul—remember, broadly accepted even by skeptics as written in the fifties of the first century—corroborates the word of Jesus to the apostle Peter and shows the flawed nature of Leigh Teabing's supposition: "The rock on which Jesus built His Church ... was not *Peter* ... It was Mary Magdalene" (248). Again, we are dealing here with "fact-ion."

Here are a few more reasons to believe that a canon was part of the church. From the beginning:

- "words of ... prophecy" (Revelation 1:3) were read in public worship along with the Old Testament texts and thus had canonical authority in the churches (Colossians 4:16);

- Paul's writings were referred to as "Scriptures" by the apostle Peter (2 Peter 3:16);

- Paul referred to the Gospel of Luke as "Scripture" (1 Timothy 5:18; see also Luke 10:7);

- Paul used the word *kanon* ("rule") when referring to the fundamental teaching of the apostles, which was to be followed and obeyed (Galatians 6:16).

The writings of the next generation of believers confirmed this understanding of the New Testament as Scripture. Ignatius of Antioch (A.D. 35–107), Polycarp (A.D. 69–115), the Epistle of Barnabas (A.D. 120), and Second Clement (A.D. 140), all referred to various New Testament books as "Scripture." According to one Dutch scholar, even the Gnostic Gospel of Truth (A.D. 140–150, doubtless known at Rome when Marcion taught there) cites a body of authoritative books that is "quasi-identical with the so-called later canon of the Church."[5] This means a body of written Scripture had to have existed before any secret Gnostic Gospels appeared since one of the earliest of these "secret

✻ MIRROR WRITING

From early on, da Vinci wrote in what is called "mirror writing," that is, writing his characters from right to left. He would fill the right-hand pages of his notebooks first, then the left-hand pages. He not only wrote from right-to-left, his actual letters were written backward as well.

Da Vinci did not do this in order to hide information or as part of some trickery or deceit. Rather, he may have had some form of dyslexia or other difficulty with perception.

gospels" had to recognize the orthodox Canon in its very attempt to redefine the Christian faith. "Before the [New Testament] books could be used ... in the *Gospel of Truth*," says the above-mentioned scholar, "they must have already enjoyed such authority for a considerable time ... all this took place before the condemnation of Marcion."[6]

Two versions of Christianity did not develop simultaneously alongside each other, as *The Da Vinci Code* maintains. That would mean the church was born in total confusion with no clear, earth-changing message. Common sense demands that there was first orthodoxy, cemented by written, widely accepted texts produced by the first generation of believers. Then there was a deviant version followed by its own set of writings.

A written canon existed at the very beginning of the Christian faith. In fact, the early church already possessed the Canon of the Old Testament. And as they wrote the New Testament, they were consciously writing the conclusion to the Canon—the fulfillment of the Old Testament. The next generation received the New Testament this way.

The New Testament Canon is not the invention of Constantine in the fourth century. It is an essential part of the teaching of Jesus and His apostles from the start. In the first century the Canon was in organic form and functioned without formal church declarations. But the orthodoxy of the twenty-seven books was there, in principle, from the beginning. Christianity and the Bible cannot be separated.

The New Testament Canon is not the invention of Constantine in the fourth century.

If the Bible is truly the Word of God, as it claims to be, then Christians who claim to be followers of that God stake everything on it. It has been said, "The church did not create the Canon: the Canon created the church." In other words, it is the Word of God from the outside, given at key moments in history through His chosen messengers, that calls the people of God into existence. In the fourth century, the church merely published for the sake of clarity what it had always believed to be true.

AN UNLIKELY UNANIMITY

You have probably played what the English call "bush telephone," known in the United States as simply "telephone." The first person whispers something like, "My older brother has three big front teeth." The message travels around the circle, and the last person triumphantly shouts, "Maya told Sisera to eat more beef." Keeping the church "on message" was a lot more difficult than playing bush telephone.

As we have noted, on the first day of the church's history, the Gospel was preached to representatives from almost every nationality—in their own languages (Acts 2:1–11). And the message spread. The church grew numerically and geographically at a phenomenal rate. Apostles scattered in all directions—Paul traveled to the Middle East and then to Europe; John went to Asia Minor; Matthew remained in Palestine; and Thomas perhaps went to India. The list goes on.

While the New Testament gives clear voice to the unity of the early church, as time passed and the church spread throughout the known world, it is understandable that not everyone had immediate access to all the books that constituted the Canon as it was at the beginning or as it was finally established. The early church was spread across vast distances, separated by months of travel, and often forced underground by persecution. It had no faxes, no telephones, no Internet, no TV, no radio. Had the early Canon not been well established very early in the church's history, it would never have survived as such an amazingly unified structure.

It is not surprising to find minor differences in the understanding of the Canon. It is surprising, however, to find such unanimity of opinion. The logistics of establishing and keeping a list of authoritative books boggles the mind. They had to be assembled more or less at the beginning of the church. Later would have been too late.

A.D. 200

Most of the New Testament was never questioned. By A.D. 200 two categories of books existed:

Those books always and everywhere accepted.

In this group were the four Gospels, the letters of Paul, and the book of Acts. These books make up four-fifths of the New Testament and were received without question by the whole church. The four Gospels—Matthew, Mark, Luke, and John—had a special place in the church from the earliest days as eyewitness accounts of the life of Jesus.

- A canon list called the Muratorian Fragment is dated to the latter half of the second century because Marcion is mentioned as a contemporary of the author. With the exception of Hebrews, James, and 1 and 2 Peter, it includes references to all the New Testament books (including the four Gospels, by name or by inference).

- The four Gospels are an interesting case. A Greek manuscript known as P45 and dated around A.D. 200, has all four Gospels together. The Magdelen College Greek Fragments of Matthew's Gospel is an early book that contains only the four biblical Gospels. One scholar argues that this collection comes from the first half of the second century.[7] Another, basing his arguments on ancient writing forms, dates it as early as the first century.[8] Whatever the case, some solid recent scholarship pushes the four Gospels much further back than what many had previously believed.

- A German scholar believes that the titles, "the Gospel according to Mark, to Matthew," and so forth, were added when the Gospels were first completed and circulated together, "between 69 and 100."[9] He reasons that if scribes had added the titles later (in the second or third centuries), there would be no way to explain the surprising fact that in the thousands of Greek manuscripts the Gospels all have the same titles.[10]

Those books still questioned in some areas.

These included 1 and 2 Peter; 1, 2, and 3 John; Jude; Revelation; James; and Hebrews. These books had the respect of the churches in certain regions, but were not accepted universally during the second century, when communication was difficult. Regional differences were the natural result of particular traditions and temporary differences rather than a refusal to recognize a unified Canon. Gradually, as this fifth of the books became better known, they too were accepted.

A.D. 200 to A.D. 400

By A.D. 200, 1 Peter and 1 John were accepted generally; Hebrews was accepted by the Eastern, but not the Western church. Origen accepted 2 Peter, James, Jude, and Hebrews, but still had doubts about 2 and 3 John.

When Constantine converted to Christianity and made it the faith of the Empire, fear of persecution disappeared. Instead, the church had imperial assistance and could convoke universal councils to discuss doctrine and deal with heretical challenges. These councils also brought order to the church's beliefs concerning the New Testament. Around A.D. 350 emerged the first universal decrees of the church concerning the Canon. In 350 the synod of Laodicea recognized all the books of the New Testament except Revelation.

Around A.D. 400, the ecumenical synods of Hippo Regius and of Carthage adopted the position recommended by Athanasius, reaffirmed in 417 when Pelagius spoke of the twenty-seven books of the New Testament as canonical and as accepted by the whole church.

The Apocryphal Books

During this period there were three types of apocryphal books; that is, books whose origins were questioned:

1. The writings of apostolic and post-apostolic fathers (late first and second centuries)
2. Popular third-class literary entertainment (second and third centuries)
3. Heretical books, especially of a Gnostic nature (second to fourth centuries)

The writings of the so-called apostolic fathers.

For years the writings of the post-apostolic fathers, that is, the generation following the New Testament times, graced the shelves of local church libraries, and some local churches seemed to treat them as canonical. The books themselves don't claim apostolic authority, and they don't have the theological power of the New Testament books. The only post-apostolic writings of great theological value are the letters of Ignatius, bishop of Antioch. But Ignatius belonged to a later period than the books of the New Testament, which he consistently recognized as his own canonical authority.

The theology of Ignatius (which stressed the central importance of each local bishop) pleased the second- and third-century church. But the church never tried to make these writings canonical—because it was determined to recognize as canonical only those books written by eyewitnesses.

Popular third-class entertainment.

The theological "soaps" of the post-apostolic church (second and third centuries) were never considered for canonical status. They included such delectable morsels as The Gospel of Nicodemus, The Acts of Pilate, the Proto-Gospel of James, and the History of the Childhood of Thomas. In this popular literature, speculation concerning the boy Jesus ran amok saying, for instance, that as a very young child, Jesus played with His friends on the bank of a river. Like the other kids, He made mud pies, but when *He* threw them in the air, they flew off as birds.

No one had the authority to call in every last copy to make the necessary alterations.

Heretical literature, especially the Gnostic texts.

The Da Vinci Code calls these books "secret gospels." They were never considered canonical because the church recognized how far they were from the message of the canonical books. *The Da Vinci Code* suggests that the church was dishonest in its method of discernment. The novel puts these words into the mouth of Teabing: "[M]ore than *eighty* gospels were considered for the New Testament, and yet only a relative few were chosen for inclusion—Matthew, Mark, Luke and John"(231).

None of the books in the three categories mentioned above fits in the canonical collection. As a religious scholar of a previous era, Kurt Aland, affirmed, "It cannot be said of a single writing preserved to us from the early period of the Church outside the New Testament that it could be properly added to the canon."[11]

WERE EARLY ACCOUNTS CONFISCATED AND BURNED?

The eccentric Teabing, supposing great expertise in the matter, states, "Constantine commissioned and financed a new Bible, which omitted those gospels that spoke of Christ's *human* traits and embellished those gospels that made Him godlike. The earlier gospels were outlawed, gathered up, and burned" (234).

There is no evidence that the text of the original Gospels was "embellished" in the fourth century. Scores and scores of copies of these Gospels already existed in the second century, establishing the text that was received in the fourth. There was no way the texts could have been altered. No one had the authority to call in from the very limits of the Empire every last copy (which by the fourth century were numbering in the hundreds, perhaps thousands) to make the necessary alterations. This really *is* fiction. More than that, it is a cheap shot at the essence of the Christian message.

Perhaps at this point your reaction to this book is "Cool it!

It's only fiction." But consider some of the typical reactions one can find posted on the Internet:

- *"The Da Vinci Code* presents thought-provoking, new, true-to-life facts and theories contradicting certain widely accepted establishments in the world."
- Or, from a teacher, "This book will make you question the clarity of Christianity as it has been known for hundreds of years."

Fiction or not, people want facts.

The church established the Canon only in the sense of identifying publicly those books that from the earliest times had already imposed themselves on the faith of believers as intrinsically canonical. There were no canonical books written in the fourth century, nor were texts embellished in the fourth century. Again Kurt Aland, one of the editors of the most widely used Greek New Testament today, sizes up the situation: "[The canon] was not imposed from the top, be it by bishops or synods, and then accepted by the communities … The organized church did not create the canon; it recognized the canon that had been created."[12]

When Christians were no longer persecuted and the Empire was at peace, the leaders of the far-flung church were finally able to meet together. When they did, they were not creating the Bible but merely clarifying and unifying once and for all what had been true from the beginning.

To determine what was canonical they asked a few simple questions:

1. Of the few books still in question, which ones agreed with the system of doctrine of the core books already unanimously accepted as canonical? That system of doctrine included the Old Testament, which shows God to be the transcendent Creator and Redeemer. It also included the history of Jesus: His birth, death, and resurrection.

2. As historical witness to Jesus, which of the books in question were from the earliest church, from the pens of the apostles and their fellow workers?

3. Did these books have the same "ring of truth" and the mark of the inspiration of the Holy Spirit as the others? This question might seem subjective, but it was not an attempt to impose a book as "inspired" so much as to recognize books that had imposed themselves by their intrinsic inspiration to canonical in the life of the church. More so, it is a matter of faith that God's Holy Spirit would have guided in their discerning what had likewise been inspired by Him—if God inspired His Word, He also protected it.

SEPARATE FACT FROM FICTION

There is a real danger today that, in the name of spiritual openness and inclusiveness, we can end up embracing the irrational and the contradictory—arguably, isn't this the real "blinding ignorance" we should be warned of from *The Da Vinci Code*? Perhaps this is even why some find themselves drawn more to the Gnostic writings—with their intrinsic ambiguities and incoherence—over and above the original, utterly coherent, consistent, and life-giving message of the authentic New Testament.

The history of the Bible is clear and open. Orthodoxy has survived great difficulties, long separations, and intense persecution through courageous preaching, holy living, martyrdom, and the life-changing power of the Gospel. *The Da Vinci Code*, and the majority scholarship that stands behind it, seeks to impose another version of history—a history of suspicion. The Hollywood star, Mel Gibson, in speaking about his movie, *The Passion of the Christ*, gets it right: "Critics who have a problem with me don't really have a problem with me in this film. They have a problem with the four Gospels."[13] People's problem with the message of the Bible forces them to reinterpret or rewrite history.

In the new version of history presented by Brown, power-hungry bishops with political aims strategically take over the church and create a Bible in the image of their personal theological choices. But the story of the Canon will not allow such a twisting of history. The New Testament functioned with minor variations from the beginning as the Canon/Rock on which Jesus promised to build His church. That church has always believed in a Gospel "once delivered unto the saints" (Jude 1:3 KJV) at a specific moment in history when God spoke definitively and uniquely through His Son (Hebrews 1:1–2).

This is the life-changing good news of God's act for lost sinners. Orthodoxy follows a straight line from the teaching of Jesus in the thirties to the writings of Paul and the other apostles in the latter half of the first century, to the final decrees of the ecumenical synods in the fifth century, seeking to preserve this original unique truth.

The Da Vinci Code uses a fictional structure to get its own message across. While seeming to advocate a courageous search for truth at any price, its real goal is to erode one of the fundamental characteristics of the Christian faith—the belief that the original message of the Gospel, enshrined in the Bible, is the unique, inspired word from God Himself, without which we are lost. + � THER THINGS

One more element, the Bible as God's Word and unique message of salvation, is erased from the Arc.

⟫◈⟪

CHAPTER 7

Is it true that "more than *eighty* gospels were considered for the New Testament" but were turned down by the church and then destroyed (231)?

Is it true that these gospels, part of an ancient library of Coptic Scrolls found near the village of Nag Hammadi, Egypt, in 1945, "highlight glaring discrepancies and fabrications ... [of] the modern Bible" (234)?

Is it true that these scrolls are "the earliest Christian records" (245)?

Is it true that "the early Church literally *stole* Jesus from His original followers, hijacking His human message, shrouding it in an impenetrable cloak of divinity" (233)?

Is it true that in the "secret gospels" genuine spiritual seekers can find the true Jesus (234)?

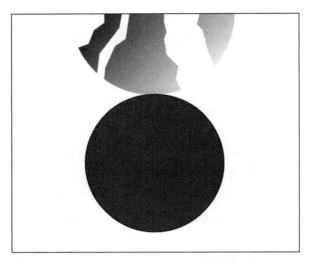

The recycled Gnostic myth that animates today's
spiritual quest erases one more essential element
of the Divine Arc.

THE GNOSTIC GOSPELS VS. THE NEW TESTAMENT GOSPELS

The scrolls highlight glaring historical discrepancies and fabrications, clearly confirming that the modern Bible was compiled and edited by men who possessed a political agenda — to promote the divinity of the man Jesus Christ and use his influence to solidify their own power base. (234)

"I don't mind your using our room, Jen. It's just that I thought we had agreed we would ask each other before we made any special plans like this." Just last night, Carrie had to leave their room for a few hours when Jen came in with her newest friend.

"Yeah, but this is really important."

"What kind of 'surprise' is this going to be?" Carrie never knew what to expect from Jen.

"Next week will be an interactive session, Carrie. Enough talking about the spirituality Brown writes about. Let's experience it. Let's experience the fullness of God for ourselves."

"You mean, like God—in the Bible?" Carrie had not yet opened the book Evan had left on a table at their meeting the night before.

"Carrie, don't you realize it yet? There is no 'God of the Bible.' That is a man-made response to the threat truth represented to them. The true god is not some male creature that is hungry for blood. Sin did not originate with a woman eating an apple. The

Bible has controlled us long enough. Now we know how to reach god ourselves without some church or priest or outdated book telling us what we can and cannot do. Next week, we will experience it ourselves, right here in this room."

As she made her way to her Women in Literature class, Carrie was still wondering what kind of interactive session Jen had planned. She had registered for the class because she wanted to see women characters be something more than empty-headed novelty items next to the handsome leading man.

"Today," said Professor Gibson, "we are going to look at some fairly new, yet very ancient, books." This apparent contradiction got Carrie's attention. "These ancient texts are contemporary with the New Testament"—*There it is again,* thought Carrie. *The Bible. Why does it keep coming up in conversation?*—"but we didn't know of their existence until 1945. These fifty-two books, or scrolls, were found near the Egyptian village of Nag Hammadi. A library of works—not just one man's way of thinking.

"These texts show a decisively different picture of women than the one painted in the Bible. Oh, the main characters are still there—Jesus, His disciples, and Mary Magdalene. But the roles are far different from what we have read before. Especially for Mary. Mary, whom the church has made out to be a whore, was actually the wife of Jesus."

Carrie looked up sharply to see if her teacher was kidding. Gibson would often say something totally off-the-wall just to see if her students were paying attention. This time, Carrie could see she was not joking.

Gibson continued talking about the scrolls found at Nag Hammadi and how scientists and archaeologists were able to verify their age. She talked about the culture and customs of the day and how these texts must have created quite a stir. She concluded,

"Maybe that is why someone thought to hide them away—so the men running the new Christian cult wouldn't find them and destroy them."

"Lucky for us someone found them," said Michelle from the back row.

"You're right, Michelle. And since we have them, we need to enjoy them." Gibson went on to assign enough "enjoyment" to keep Carrie and her classmates busy for many hours. They were told to read from the Gospel of Philip and the Gospel of Mary, then to submit a paper contrasting the Mary in the Bible with the Mary in the Nag Hammadi texts.

"I think you will begin to get a much clearer picture," said Gibson as she wrapped up the class, "of how women can be portrayed in literature when Christians aren't involved."

———————

What if they have really discovered earth-shaking truths in these texts that were suppressed but have now been rediscovered?

Is it true that "more than *eighty* gospels were considered for the New Testament" but were turned down by the church and then destroyed (231)?

Is it true that these gospels, part of an ancient library of Coptic Scrolls found near the village of Nag Hammadi, Egypt, in 1945, "highlight glaring discrepancies and fabrications ... [of] the modern Bible" (234)?

Is it true that these scrolls are "the earliest Christian records" (245)?

Is it true that "many scholars claim that the early Church literally *stole* Jesus from His original followers, hijacking His human message, shrouding it in an impenetrable cloak of divinity, and using it to expand their own power" (233)?

Is it true that in the "secret gospels" genuine spiritual seekers can find the *true* Jesus (234)?

It is all true, *if* one can believe the reassuringly handsome and intelligent Robert Langdon, Harvard professor of religious symbology, who—with his courageous, bright, and beautiful co-fugitive, Sophie Neveu—is on a search for truth wherever it may be found.

I (Peter) know a real-life equivalent to Robert Langdon. As I sat in that Harvard research seminar room, I caught sight of the beautiful and brilliant Elaine Pagels. At the time, she was twenty-four and a rising star, one of the privileged handful of scholars to be included in a group studying those Nag Hammadi Gnostic texts that no one else had yet seen.

A handful of radical New Testament scholars have sought to pull off a palace revolution.

Pagels is now the Harrington Spear Paine Professor of Religion at Princeton University, and she has lived both a star-spangled life and a tragic life. She has become a world-class scholar, but she lost a husband to a mountaineering accident and a young child to illness. She writes freely about these losses and about her spiritual quest.

Pagels' book, *The Gnostic Gospels*, published when she was thirty-five, was an immediate best-seller. Almost single-handedly, it moved the lost Nag Hammadi texts, perhaps the real heroes of *The Da Vinci Code*, from the ivory tower into the public square.[1] Writing with "the instincts of a novelist," as one reviewer said, she brought the Gnostic heretics to life and made them likeable. She presented Gnosticism (a religion of self-

The founder of the Jesus Seminar has vowed to take the "new scholarship" to the masses.

knowledge and of deep spiritual experience) as an alternate expression of early Christianity—the same story told from another side. To her, the Gnostic "Christians" are the forgotten victims and heroes of a class war waged by the politically powerful bishops.

A generation of scholars studied the fifty-two Coptic scrolls, only five of which are called "gospels," and produced an English translation in 1977.[2] Since that time, a handful of radical—some would say extremist—New Testament scholars associated with a group called the Jesus Seminar have sought to pull off a "palace revolution." In one generation, they have used these scrolls to

- redefine Jesus,
- rewrite the origins of the Christian faith,
- rewrite early church history,
- redefine the contents of the Canon, and
- completely reinterpret the Christian faith as a particular version of "Gnostic" spirituality.

Radical religious feminism has also found in these long-lost texts a gold mine of inspiration to recreate reality in the likeness of the "sacred feminine." The leader at the 1997 Gathering of Presbyterian Women ceremoniously laid the Bible aside and asked the 5,300 participants to consider new revelations—women's diaries and the "new" gospels, since the four Gospels of the Bible were full of male, human bias.

The founder of the Jesus Seminar has vowed to take the "new scholarship" to the masses. With the publication of *The Da Vinci Code*, it has happened. Now many are asking if these "secret gospels" are the earliest, most authentic expression of original Christianity.

Is all this true? Have we been duped for centuries, and must we now be willing to give up faith in a shattered dream? Is the new version of Jesus where our true allegiance belongs? To answer these crucial questions, we must address three underlying issues:

1. How early are these scrolls?
2. What do they teach?
3. Why is this teaching so attractive right now?

How Early Are the Coptic Scrolls?

A few recognized scholars today claim that one of these "secret gospels," the Gospel of Thomas, is the second earliest Christian writing in existence, earlier than Matthew, Mark, Luke, and John. Yet, the scholars who first began studying these documents didn't seem to make such claims. One expert on the Gospel of Thomas said in 1961, "[The Gospel of Thomas's] character is so far removed from the four canonical Gospels that it cannot be put on a par with them."[3]

So how do these recent scholars make their novel case? They use a strange argument based on a document mentioned in *The Da Vinci Code*, a scroll called "Q." This is a little hard to explain, and it is so obscure that we would rather not try. However, scholars have completely redefined Christianity on the basis of "Q," so bear with us as we attempt to explain it as clearly as possible.

Scholars looked at Matthew's Gospel and Luke's Gospel and noticed that long sections of the material were identical. So they examined only that shared material, setting aside the rest. They noticed that the

> *No one has ever found the "Q" scroll.*

shared material does not speak about the death and resurrection of Jesus. "Aha," they thought. "This means that both Matthew and Luke must have been using another scroll, from which they copied the material."

No one has ever found such a scroll. As far as anyone knows, it doesn't exist. But, having guessed it into existence, the scholars called it "Q" and argued that it had to be earlier than either Matthew or Luke. In fact, they said, "Q" has to be the earliest Christian writing. From these extracted verses made into a book, these scholars then made up a new picture of Jesus. They argued that the earliest followers of Jesus used this book as their only scripture and did not believe in the "later" picture of Jesus we get from the biblical Gospels.

Because the Gospel of Thomas is similar in nature to the non-existent book "Q" (not mentioning the death and resurrection, for example), it too must be one of the earliest books about Jesus and the true way to understand who He is.

Where Is "Q"?

There are two major problems here. First, no one has ever seen "Q." It is a creation that exists purely in the minds of scholars. There was no manuscript named "Q" found in the sands of Egypt... or anywhere else.

Speaking of Egypt, imagine the solidity of those great pyramids built 4,500 years ago. Now imagine that you could turn one of them upside down and balance its enormous weight on one small stone slab in the hot Egyptian sand. It might stand for a day or two before it toppled of its own weight. This is what we are being asked to believe about "Q" and the Gospel of Thomas. The two-thousand-year-old edifice of the Christian faith has been turned upside down and is now balanced on one hypothetical document no one has ever seen!

Second, there is no need for "Q" to exist at all. There is a very simple explanation for the shared material in Matthew and Luke: as he wrote his Gospel, Luke used material from Matthew's Gospel as a faithful witness about certain things.

Which Really Came First?

Not one other scroll dug up along with the Gospel of Thomas has ever been dated so early. It apparently cannot be done; otherwise some scholar in the Gnostic camp would have tried it. The early case for a "Gnostic" Jesus stands or falls with the Gospel of Thomas. All the books of the New Testament can be plausibly dated prior to A.D. 70.[4] The earliest likely date for the Nag Hammadi scrolls is around A.D. 150 and later, when Gnosticism as a system began to flourish. This date is accepted for the Gospel of Philip, which has Jesus kissing Mary Magdalene on the lips, and for the Gospel of Mary, which claims a leading role for Mary Magdalene. *The Da Vinci Code* draws its Holy Grail myth partly from these two gospels, claiming that they also predated the Gospels that now appear in our New Testament.

In our last chapter we met Marcion, "the Mouse that roared." In spite of himself, Marcion nibbled away not only at the biblical Gospels but at early dates for the Gnostic texts. The New Testament mentions that "false teachers" are coming, generally of a Gnostic kind.[5] Half-baked forms of Gnosticism were already emerging when the apostle Peter wrote of "cleverly devised

The Gnostic Gospels

In December, 1945, near the Egyptian town of Nag Hammadi, a peasant came across a number of ancient scrolls and texts. The texts, dating back to the fourth century, include poems, myths, mysticism, and what scholars call "secret gospels."

These secret gospels include:

The Gospel of Thomas
The Gospel of Philip
The Gospel of Truth
The Gospel to the Egyptians
The Apocalypse of Peter
The Apocalypse of Paul
The Letter of Peter to Philip
The Thunder, Perfect Mind
Testimony of Truth

It is in the Testimony of Truth that we read the Garden of Eden scene from the point of view of the serpent. God is made out to be a jealous, raging man while the serpent is seen as the speaker of divine wisdom.

myths" (2 Peter 1:16ff ESV) that would threaten Christian faithfulness to historic, divine revelation.

Historians call Marcion a "proto-Gnostic" because his system was not nearly as developed as those that appeared in the second century and produced the kind of literature discovered in Nag Hammadi. Such books were scarce in Marcion's day. Marcion did not cite the Gospel of Truth, and it is passing strange that he didn't cite the Gospel of Thomas, if indeed it was the original gospel. Marcion could have based his whole argument on this so-called original teaching of Jesus, since it would have fit so perfectly with what Marcion taught.

Two versions of Christianity did not develop alongside each other, as *The Da Vinci Code* maintains. The first message was the Christian message from Jesus and His apostles, established through widely accepted texts written by the first generation of believers. Later, there was a reactionary message, Gnostic heresy, which was cemented by its own set of writings.

The Christian chicken came before the Gnostic egg.

WHAT DO THE SCROLLS TEACH?

Original Christianity had a very particular understanding of religious truth based on two elements:

1. First was eyewitness testimony of God's special intervention in human affairs by those divinely appointed for the task. For instance, the apostle Peter claimed to have seen with his physical eyes the divine glory of

Jesus the Son of God at the "transfiguration" (2 Peter 1:16 ESV) when His clothing turned radiantly white (see also Matthew 17:1–8; Mark 9:2–8; Luke 9:28–36).

2. To this eyewitness testimony was added the witness of inspired written Old Testament Scripture. Peter wrote, "So [now] we have the prophetic message [the Old Testament] more fully confirmed" (2 Peter 1:19 ESV).

[handwritten margin notes: Spirituality above history SPIRITUALITY w/o GOD / Materiality in history RELIGION w/o GOD]

Gnostic Myth

Myths are human stories and fables about the spiritual nature of the world. In that sense, the Gnostic Gospel writers were interested in spirituality above history, because Gnostics believed that spiritual experience was the source of religious truth. Marcion, for instance, preached about the "Alien God," who is not to be confused with the God of the Old Testament. One needs to ask, how alien is this spirituality to that of the Bible?

In this book there is not enough space to discuss this subject, but suffice it to say, it's amazing to discover just what is in those secret, supposedly life-giving "gospels." While the "secret gospels" differ from and contradict one another, they share the same orientation. The collection functions suspiciously like a Gnostic canon that has deliberately excluded anything of a biblical

The Gnostic is free from biblical law because the foolish Yahweh made up the law.

Christian nature. Apparently, power-hungry Christian bishops were not the only ones discriminating against notions they did not approve.

Gnostic texts despise sexual distinctions, marriage, and motherhood.

The most striking theme common to all fifty-two texts dug up at Nag Hammadi is the rejection of the Genesis creation account. The Gnostic texts constantly mock the Creator God as a blind fool. Jahweh is the first and mightiest of all oppressive patriarchs. He is the "heavenly" counterpart of all blustering macho brutes who think they know everything because they are male.

These texts despise all created things, especially sexual distinctions, marriage, and motherhood. The true believer must be liberated from such earthly constraints. The Gnostic is also free from any law because the foolish Jahweh made up the law. In this way of thinking, there is no sin, the fall of Genesis 3 is *liberation*, and the serpent of the garden speaks wisdom. The Gnostic Jesus comes with the same message—not to free us from our sin, but to free us from our ignorance. We do not know who we really are. He brings us *gnosis*: knowledge. The knowledge is this—we are divine.

"The Latest Paganism"

Is this kind of thinking simply another valid form of Christianity that was deliberately suppressed by closed-minded, control-obsessed bigots in the fourth century? Duncan Greenlees has the answer. Greenlees is a modern Gnostic from the theosophical/occult tradition and has no desire to be associated with

Christianity. His evaluation of Gnosticism offers an objective and surprising answer to our question:

> Gnosticism is a system of direct experiential knowledge of God … the Soul and the universe; … in the early centuries of this era, amid a growing Christianity, it took on the form of the Christian faith, while rejecting most of its specific beliefs. Its wording is therefore largely Christian, while *its spirit is that of the latest paganism of the West* [emphasis added].[6]

BLUE WORDS/YELLOW MEANING

FAITHFUL CONSTRAINTS

WHY IS GNOSTICISM SO ATTRACTIVE TODAY?

Because these ancient Gnostic scrolls are so anti-biblical, they cannot be, as Greenlees confirms, an alternate form of original Christianity. *The Da Vinci Code* clouds over this fact, but a clear analysis shows two contradictory religious belief systems—characterized by the two antagonistic "Gods" of Marcion. At least Marcion was honest: It's an either/or situation. If one is true, the other is false; they cannot both be true at the same time.

How objective is the scholarship of the fictional Langdon and of the very real Pagels? How much is it driven by a religious agenda? Do these texts—the ancient scrolls, this modern novel, and contemporary pro-Gnostic academic scholarship—all serve a religious commitment that goes far beyond a simple search for historical truth?

Brown's book is, as the French say, "the drop that makes the glass overflow" (or as English puts it, "the straw that breaks the camel's back"). With the appearance of *The Da Vinci Code*, related books such as those of Pagels on the ancient Gnostic texts are flying off bookstore shelves faster than they can be stocked—but for reasons much deeper than the success of a page-turner novel.

These Gnostic writings have reappeared at a time when patriarchy, doctrinal precision, canons, confessions, clearly defined sexual morality, church institutions, and authority are out. What's in? The personal spiritual quest, diversity, individualism, egalitarianism, and sexual liberation. And the prospect of finding ancient "Christian" scrolls that support this new era's spiritual viewpoint is, for many post-moderns, a dream come true.

The Best of Both Worlds?

Here we begin to decipher *The Da Vinci Code* and to suggest the real reason for its enormous popularity. The book appeals to many people because it expresses in such an engrossing way the new liberating religious option that has recently taken the West by storm.

The generation of the 1960s broke down all the "repressive" sexual rules and went east to Katmandu for spiritual reassurance. They came back with good news: You can be spiritual and still be sexually active in all kinds of ways.

Now you can save your airfare twice over. You don't have to follow the Beatles east. The East with its gurus, its spirituality, and its yoga, has come west, and you can be a "new" kind of Christian who keeps the best of both worlds.

The Da Vinci Code is a powerful form of religious propaganda. In an interview on ABC's *20/20* Dan Brown spoke about his "conversion" to a new way of thinking about the origins of Christianity. He also admitted that he saw himself as being on a mission to bring this religious message to mainstream America.

At a different level, scholar Elaine Pagels is on a similar mission. Pagels was once an evangelical Christian, but she now says she is "quite enchanted ... and delighted by" a woman who was the head of a Gnostic church in Palo Alto, California.[7] In an interview on National Public Radio she admitted to a fascination with the Gnostic texts, especially *Thunder, Perfect Mind*. This text praises a female personification of the divine, who identifies herself as Isis, the Egyptian goddess.

Peter, Paul, and John warned the early church of seductive myths in "Christian" apparel.

Thunder says in typical, all-inclusive prose, "I am the prostitute and the holy one, ... the wife and the virgin, ... knowledge and ignorance, ... bride and bridegroom, ... shame and shamelessness."[8] Recently Pagels found a spiritual home in the Church of the Heavenly Rest in New York, led by a "woman priest," where she was able to reject the notion that being a Christian was "synonymous with accepting a set of beliefs" such as the Apostles' Creed. Pagels is also interested in the blending of Christianity and Buddhism.[9] A number of the Jesus Seminar scholars, having also freed themselves from biblical orthodoxy, are on a similar religious mission.

The prophet Isaiah had to warn Israel of the temptation to blend biblical faith with other religions. Peter, Paul, and John warned the early church of seductive myths in "Christian" apparel. The church must now warn Christians against new (but oh, so old) "clever" myths about the nature of the world.

All good myths are cleverly devised, to borrow the apostle Peter's term. Nothing is simple. We must keep all our wits about us in this debate about truth. The Bible warns us with great clarity that there is a huge distinction between these two forms of religious knowing:

- *Revelation*, which was inspired by the transcendent Lord, the Creator and Redeemer of the heavens and the earth, and

- *Myths*, which have a non-inspired, human, or cultural source.

The recycled Gnostic myth that animates today's spiritual quest erases one more essential element of the Divine Arc.

CHAPTER 8

Is it true that sex is "a mystical, spiritual act ... [whereby one can] find that spark of divinity that man can only achieve through union with the sacred feminine" (310)?

Is it true that the "Hieros Gamos [sacred marriage] ritual is not a perversion ... [but] a deeply sacrosanct ceremony" used by the early church (309)?

Is it true that androgyny (the fusion of male and female in one person) is a valid goal of Christian spirituality?

Is it true that all spirituality is equally valid, as *The Da Vinci Code* often seems to suggest?

In its bold invitation to earth-centered spirituality,
The Da Vinci Code erases one more piece from the
Divine Arc.

SECRET KNOWLEDGE

*Our ancient heritage and our very physiologies tell us sex is natural—
a cherished route to spiritual fulfillment—and yet modern religion decries
it as shameful, teaching us to fear our sexual desire as
the hand of the devil (310).*

Carrie was not a fan, to say the least, of Biology 101. She had
put off the mandatory course until her senior year, hoping that the
requirement would change. It hadn't, and now she was gritting
her teeth and giving the least amount of effort she could in order
to pass.

To make things worse, her lab partner had to change their lab to
Tuesday night—right when Carrie's reading group for *The Da Vinci
Code* was meeting. Carrie's roommate, Jen, had promised a surprise
for tonight, and Carrie was going to have to hurry through this lab in
order to make it for even half of the time.

"Wow, Carrie," said her lab partner, Becka. "You seem more
preoccupied than usual. I know you hate Bio, but could you snap
out of it for a few minutes so we can finish this?" Their project
that night was counting fruit flies, separating the male and female
flies.

"I'm sorry, Becka. I'm supposed to be someplace else right now,
and I'm thinking about that."

"Big party, huh? On a Tuesday?"

"No, not a party. I'm sorry—I'll try to concentrate."

She put her eye against the optical element of the microscope and moved the slide, counting aloud. She kept this up through three slides, then asked Becka if she could take over the counting. "This is giving me a headache," said Carrie.

"Honestly, Carrie—I like you and all, but you're useless tonight. Why don't you just go to your party and let me do this." Becka was a sophomore Pre-Med major who loved Biology as much as Carrie disliked it.

Carrie didn't try to correct Becka about the party. "Thanks, Becka. I'll try to make it up to you." She shoved her books into her backpack and walked quickly toward her dorm. As she neared her room, she heard what sounded like singing. No, not singing. It was more like chanting.

Carrie opened the door and was greeted with a true surprise.

All the lights were out, yet shadows were cast on the wall by some unseen source. There were nine women—no, eight women and Jay—standing in a circle, facing inward. Carrie walked further into the room and closed the door quietly behind her. Jen was speaking.

"The Great Goddess is here with us tonight. She is personal, earthy, tangible, real. She is substantive. She is in our midst in the form of our bodies. We call her name."

The other women in the circle called out names in turn.

"Isis!"

"Tara!"

"Eve!"

"Asherah!"

"Mary!"

Jen had her arms wrapped around her midsection. She called out, "The sacred feminine resides in me. She resides in my belly, my innermost being."

Carrie could see that a candle was burning in the middle of the circle. By that light she saw Jen pulling up her shirt enough to reveal some sort of marking on her belly.

"The circle is the sign of the sacred feminine. Completeness. Wholeness. We stand in a circle to honor that which is sacred, that which lives inside of us. We are the circle. Draw the sacred circle on your belly." Each of the participants took turns using a marker to draw a circle around their belly buttons.

Then Jen lifted her hands above her head and began chanting, "Mary! Madonna! Eve! Isis! We call your name. You are welcome in us. We receive you in your wholeness to fill us, fulfill us. We are the sacred feminine!" She began to dance slowly, in an ever-widening circle. The others joined in, swaying, dancing, chanting the names of the sacred feminine over and over. Jen opened her eyes and saw Carrie standing at the door. When Jen held her arms out to Carrie and began moving toward her, Carrie turned and, fumbling in the dark, found the door. She pulled it open and ran out into the hall, down the stairs, and outside. She was almost to the Commons before she realized it was raining.

⇒◆⇐

Reading *The Da Vinci Code* reminded me (Peter) of the week I spent at the Parliament of the World's Religions in Chicago in 1993. Eight thousand delegates were there, representing 125 different religions. We sang "Leaning on the Everlasting Arms," but the song failed to identify whose arms they were. I popped my head into the darkened "meditation room" and listened briefly to the unfamiliar chanting sounds.

I made a quick break for the exit when the leaders of the Fellowship of Isis "seminar" announced that they were about to enter "the second chamber." The first chamber was enough for me. In it the audience wailed, as if possessed, in ecstatic praise of the Goddess. The only spirituality I didn't see all week was that of biblical Christianity.

Is it true that sex is "a mystical, spiritual act ... [whereby one can] find that spark of divinity that man can only achieve through union with the sacred feminine" (310)?

Is it true that the "Hieros Gamos [sacred marriage] ritual is not a perversion ... [but] a deeply sacrosanct ceremony" used by the early church (309)?

Is it true that androgyny (the fusion of male and female in one person) is a valid goal of Christian spirituality?

Is it true that all spirituality is equally valid, as *The Da Vinci Code* often seems to suggest?

THE "SACROSANCT CEREMONY"

One of the most powerful scenes in *The Da Vinci Code* takes place in early spring in windswept Normandy. Sophie Neveu discovers her grandfather, Jacques Saunière, engaged in a secret sex ritual in the basement of his old country house, as masked worshipers look on, rocking back and forth and chanting. The men are dressed in black, the women in white. Later Robert Langdon explains to a distraught Sophie that the ritual she saw was *Hieros Gamos*, "sacred marriage," and that it was "not about sex, it was about spirituality ... not a perversion ... [but] a deeply sacrosanct ceremony" (308–309).

In this scene is found the only extended description of a religious experience in the entire novel. Here Brown illustrates "the sacred feminine."

The word *sacred* means "special" or "holy"; *feminine* in this context, stands for "goddess spirituality," which we will discuss in the next chapter. *The Da Vinci Code* explains why the rite of holy marriage fell on hard times: "Holy men who had once required sexual union with their female counterparts to commune with God now feared their natural sexual urges as the work of the devil" (125), and thus the rite was banished by the narrow-minded church.

The Gnostic Gospel of Philip (on which *The Da Vinci Code* depends for the statement that Jesus and Mary Magdalene kissed on the lips) emphasizes the spirituality of "sacred marriage." Having studied the Gospel of Philip, we agree with Brown's claim that "all descriptions of ... secret rituals in this novel [*The Da Vinci Code*] are accurate" (1). At least in this case.

The "bridal chamber" in the Gospel of Philip was reserved for secret and private initiations of "free men and virgins," who wore clothes of "perfect light." (This term is probably a euphemism for spiritual and physical nakedness.)[1] According to second-century expert on Gnosticism Irenaeus, mantras also accompanied the ceremony of the bridal chamber.[2] Early Christian teachers who witnessed this activity firsthand called it "promiscuous intercourse."[3] Here, too, *The Da Vinci Code* accurately describes a spirituality that took place in history and claimed to be true Christianity. The non-Christian pagan mysteries also had such rites of initiation. Such a ritual takes place

Feminine, in this context, stands for "goddess spirituality."

177

If this is true, then we were all wrong about the founder of Christianity.

in the basement of the home of Jacques Saunière, who "was no Christian" (140). In spite of this fact, Saunière is one of the models of spirituality in the novel.

The goal of the ritual is to gain, at the moment of orgasm in a sexual union with a woman, spiritual completeness and gnosis, or secret knowledge (308). *The Da Vinci Code* does not say how the woman gains knowledge, since she is only a "chalice" in this rite (309), but the male, with the help of the chanting crowd, "could achieve a climactic instant when his mind went totally blank and he could see God" (309). This is not a happy home and family experience in which sex produces children. Jesus' "marriage" to Mary is of the same nature—not a family but a physical union for spiritual ecstasy. From this definition of union flow a number of hair-raising implications.

A JESUS WE NEVER KNEW?

If males find spiritual knowledge through ritual orgasm with women, then the solely human Jesus described in the Gnostic texts got His knowledge of God the way all males get it—when His mind went totally blank at the moment of sexual orgasm. If this is true, then we were all wrong about the founder of Christianity. He was no more than a first-century version of the modern cult leaders we read about, who use the women around them under the pretense of spirituality.

Hippies might have approved of this Jesus, a model for extra-marital free sex. We could even sell this Jesus to testosterone-driven BMOCs (big men on campus) via campus groups called University Sexual Fellowship or Climax Crusade. Students would come to understand, with faculty advisors like Robert Langdon, that sex is "a mystical, spiritual act ... [whereby one can] find that spark of divinity that man can only achieve through union with the sacred feminine" (310). Forgive the skeptical humor ... we are only trying to show the questionable motives of this kind of spirituality.

Is *The Da Vinci Code* just an interesting "historical" novel, or is its research on these ancient practices serving a contemporary purpose? To us, the answer is obvious. The novel is making a case for an old form of spirituality that is reappearing in the twenty-first century.

A decade ago, I (Peter) wrote a book (*The Gnostic Empire Strikes Back*[4]) in which I traced the parallels between ancient Gnosticism and New Age spirituality. The term "New Age" has gone stale, but the spirituality it described has hit the religious charts as number one—thanks to books like *The Da Vinci Code*.

Someone has said, "We are not dealing with fringe religious groups ... but with a broad-based effort to influence and restructure our whole society ... 'a new society forming within the heart of

"We are witnessing the rise of a new school of mysticism [even] within Christianity."

the old.'"[5] The earth is shuddering beneath our feet. As a Roman Catholic writer states, "We are witnessing a spiritual revolution of great magnitude in the whole world ... the rise of a new school of mysticism [even] within Christianity."[6]

But why is this happening? Setting aside the cynical question of motives ... because people do yearn for spiritual transformation!

THE POST-CHRISTIAN MANTRA

In a chat room devoted to *The Da Vinci Code*, a mainline minister said, "I heard that religion is the vessel but spirituality is the holy nectar that goes in it. The nectar is what gives the religious-life life." For Jacques Saunière, transformation comes through spiritual delirium. The mind goes blank, and other sensations take over. Today we call this "altered states of consciousness." Orgasm and chanting constitute one avenue to ecstatic, mindless experience. There are many others. The hippies went on "trips" through the use of drugs, which some ancient Gnostics and many Native American rituals used. Other methods include drumming, beating sticks, bells, or gongs, rhythmic dancing, changes of breathing, and deep meditation.

A contemporary New Age teacher says, "The enemy of meditation is the mind."

Many people today equate this experience with being or feeling "spiritual." An academic discipline called "transpersonal psychology" studies and promotes these "technologies of the sacred" as the wave of our spiritual future and the only hope for the planet.[7] Apparently, what drove second-century "Christian" Gnostics is driving more and more of us. Our post-Christian culture is rediscovering this ancient spirituality. No wonder many post-moderns, increasingly even within the church, are insisting that Christianity must be made to conform to this model. After all, haven't we come to realize that such experience is common to all religions? As one writer on Jesus said, "Jesus won't become a national figure [in America] unless he can move outside Christianity."[8] The enticing promise? If we can only realize this truth, then global spiritual unity will finally be within our grasp.

The first goal of spiritual ecstasy is mindlessness, a state sought in Hindu and Buddhist meditation, often through the repetition of a "mantra." The term *mantra* comes from two Sanskrit words, *man* ("to think") and *tra* ("to be liberated from"). Loose translation: "You are

THE LAST SUPPER

Leonardo da Vinci completed his great masterpiece *The Last Supper* in 1498. The fresco began to deteriorate almost immediately. It has been repainted and restored at least seven times since da Vinci's time.

Many consider this da Vinci's crowning achievement, blending what he had learned through the years in the areas of sculpture, light, sound, and human anatomy. The result is a picture of Christ and His disciples that shows emotion like no artist had done before.

Da Vinci made countless intricate drawings of each figure, and made detailed entries in his notebook about each disciple's position and action. ("Another speaks into the ear of his neighbor, and the other who listens to him has turned to him, giving him his ear and holding a knife in one hand and in the other the half-cut piece of bread.")[9]

at your best when you are not thinking." Can you hear your children using that excuse to get out of homework?

Hinduism, the so-called path to mystical experience, involves getting beyond the intellect or "killing the mind."[10] A contemporary New Age teacher says, "The enemy of meditation is the mind."[11] The ancient Gnostics taught the same. One of the Gnostic scrolls calls for "an entry into that which is silent, the place which has no need for utterance nor for comprehending."[12] The Jesus of another Gnostic scroll commands his disciples, "Be filled with the Spirit, but be lacking in reason or intellect (*logos*)."[13]

Why the escape from the mind? The simple answer: to get life-changing knowledge (*gnosis*).

WHY IS MONA LISA SMILING?

The astute reader of *The Da Vinci Code* will notice the mention of the word *androgynous*. At the sex ritual, the cult members are wearing "androgynous masks" (308); Jahweh is presented as an ancient name containing the idea of an "androgynous physical union";[14] Leonardo da Vinci's Mona Lisa is "smiling" (101). "Why? Because Mona Lisa really stands for Amon and L'Isa (Isis), the androgynous pair, so that the painting presents an image that is "neither male nor female … [but] carries a subtle message of androgyny … a fusing of both" (121). The *Mona Lisa* smiles because she has *gnosis*.

This view of sexuality makes homosexuality normal, as *The Da Vinci Code* indicates in its celebration of da Vinci's gay identity (120). It even makes pansexuality—that is, all forms of sexuality—normal. Who can deny that this is the direction of sexual expression in the twenty-first century? Each form of sexuality comes with its own claim on spirituality.[15] If sexual orgasm is the royal way to knowledge of God, perhaps such orgasm doesn't have to occur only with a woman. Maybe, as the gays and pansexualists claim, any kind of orgasm will qualify.

THE JOINING OF THE OPPOSITES

The liberation of sex is not the only effect of such spirituality. Long before the appearance of *The Da Vinci Code*, Gnostic believers were "reconstructed in androgynous unity" in the bridal chamber.[16] In other words, something happened to them that changed the way they thought about themselves. Such transformation is the goal of all these techniques. Shirley MacLaine said the very point of life was to know ourselves as we truly are—"androgynous, a perfect balance."[17] What do Shirley MacLaine and Dan Brown know that most of us do not know?

Knowing oneself to be both male and female changes everything, according to this esoteric tradition. Reconstructing God-given sexuality appears in this spirituality to be at the top of the agenda. In undergoing this transformation, one "joins the opposites," the classic phrase for *gnosis*. This means that in the irrational state of altered consciousness, all the normal distinctions of

Each form of sexuality comes with its own claim on spirituality.

everyday life—not merely the sexual distinctions—fall away: *"The blade and chalice. Fused as one"* (446). This concept is further expressed in Jacques Saunière's "passion for dualism ... Everything in pairs ... *Male female. Black nested within white"* (323).

This is the deep Gnostic experience of liberation. As we saw in *Thunder, Perfect Mind,* a part of Gnostic spirituality, one who identifies herself as the Egyptian Goddess Isis said of herself, "I am the whore and the holy one ... the wife and the virgin ... I am the one whose wisdom is great in Egypt (Isis) ... I am sinless and the root of sin derives from me ... I am the one who is called Truth and iniquity."[18] The Gospel of Truth (mentioned in chapter 7) describes this knowledge as being swallowed up into the unity of all things.[19] The joining of the opposites means that those so joined rise above all distinctions, which are mere illusion, or, as the Hindus say, *maya.*

This, they would insist, must especially be true of what Christians traditionally distinguish as "good" and "evil."

No-Guilt "Liberation"

There is more to a Gnostic spiritual high than trance-like ecstasy or physical orgasm. There is an experience of *dominion,* a great sense of empowerment, fraught with great danger. Going beyond the limitations of your mind also takes you beyond rational definitions of right and wrong. You are no longer subject to external laws of good and evil. Instead, you become the judge. Everything about you seems okay, and all your instincts must be valid.

The ultimate goal of this mystical experience of oneness

with all things, is clear—*to deny guilt*. In this system, there is no place for sin. According to Robert Langdon, "It was *man*, not God, who created the concept of ... sin" (238).

In the 1970s, an occult "Jesus," very like the Jesus of the Gnostic Gospels, supposedly channeled messages to a Jewish atheistic psychologist, who wrote them down and published them as the New Age text, *A Course in Miracles*. This Jesus said, "Do not make the pathetic error of clinging to the old rugged cross ... Your only calling here is to devote yourself with active willingness to the denial of guilt in all its forms."[20] When you go within, notions like right and wrong, guilt and active conscience, disappear. You can become king or queen of de-nial!

This kind of "liberation" is dangerous. Bruce Davis of the Manson family, now a professing Christian, says about LSD that it "enlarged my sense of what was permissible ... the unthinkable became the thinkable and the thinkable became the doable."[21]

Mystical spirituality deadens the God-given mechanism of moral pain that alerts us to our worst selves.

By embracing evil, mystical spirituality produces a temporary, counterfeit euphoria of virtual redemption and relief from guilt. But in truth, it merely deadens the God-given mechanism of moral pain that would otherwise alert us to our worst selves.

Perhaps Brown has not thought through all the implications

of his message, but *The Da Vinci Code* is a deliberate and powerful propaganda tool for this view of spirituality.

However, in claiming that the early church used "sex to commune directly with God" (309), the novel goes too far. There is not one hint of either condoning or acknowledging—let alone encouraging—such practice in the books of the New Testament, all of which have been plausibly dated prior to A.D. 70. The case for the Gnostic texts is quite different.

> *The Gospel of Philip does not represent the spirituality of Jesus and the earliest Christianity.*

Remember (from chapter 7) that *no scholar of any particular leaning* suggests that the Gospel of Philip was written earlier than the New Testament. At the very earliest, it is dated around A.D. 175.[22] The official translator of the Gospel of Philip in the Nag Hammadi collection suggests a date of about A.D. 250.[23] The Gospel of Philip does not represent the spirituality of Jesus and the earliest Christianity. The external evidence alone insists that it had to be an extremist Gnostic perversion of both biblical spirituality and sexuality. Gnostic "Christians" were not the original thing— they sought to transform Christianity into one of the pagan mystery religions so popular in the ancient world.[24]

CHRISTIAN SPIRITUALITY

The use of secret rituals and manipulative techniques by committed followers of Christ to produce altered states of consciousness is found nowhere in the Bible. Biblical spirituality is very different from Gnostic spirituality. There are no secret chambers, no drumming, dancing, drugs, or technologies to produce altered states of consciousness. In fact, Jesus commanded that there be no babbling of mantras (Matthew 6:7). There are no secret rituals or ceremonies. On the contrary, unbelievers are openly invited to participate in the church's celebrations (1 Corinthians 14:22–25).

An exception is made for the Lord's Supper, which is for believers only. But even for this, the most intimate act of Christian fellowship, the supper was not taken in a back room, in private, accompanied by all sorts of cultic/occult activity. The tone of openness was set by Jesus, who stated, "I have spoken openly to the world. I have always taught in synagogues and in the temple, where all Jews come together. I have said nothing in secret" (John 18:20 ESV). He commanded His disciples to preach from the rooftops (Matthew 10:27).

The last line of *The Da Vinci Code* offers a radically different spirituality, far from an interesting Christian variant. Here we find ourselves in a totally different world, a world both very ancient and very modern. Robert Langdon, the heroic seeker of truth, is finally on the verge of discovering the object of his quest when he hears "a woman's voice ... the wisdom of the ages ... whispering up from the chasms of the earth" (454).

Contrast that final scene with the authentic Christian style—proclaiming to all the world a message that is

- "the open statement of the truth" (2 Corinthians 4:2 ESV);
- "not for the elite" (1 Corinthians 1:26–31);
- about events that were "not done in a corner" (Acts 26:26); and
- characterized by prayer as Jesus taught it to His disciples—praising and making requests with rational simplicity to the Father who is in heaven (Matthew 6:9–13).

In its bold invitation to earth-centered spirituality, The Da Vinci Code *erases one more piece from the Divine Arc.*

CHAPTER 9

Is it true that the symbolism in the circle is simply innocent (343)?

Is it true that Baphomet is a harmless symbol for the goodness of sexuality and another way to speak of wisdom (316–321)?

Is it true that Satan is the result of "the Church's attempts to recast the horned fertility god as a symbol of evil" to demonize its opponents (316)?

Is it true that "the Church launched a smear campaign against the pagan gods and goddesses, recasting their divine symbols as evil" (37)?

The symbol of the great Goddess, like all the other
"pre-Christian" pagan symbols esteemed by *The
Da Vinci Code* that we have examined in this chapter, erases one more huge piece from the Divine
Arc.

THE CLASH OF THE SYMBOLS

A newly emerging power [took] over the existing symbols and degrade[d]
them over time in an attempt to erase their meaning. In the battle between the
pagan symbols and the Christian symbols, the pagans lost (37).

Carrie arrived back at her dorm after two in the morning, not knowing what she would find. The room was dark and empty. There was no sign of the gathering at all. Nothing except a poster board on the wall with a large circle in the middle.

Jen was in her bed, asleep. Carrie climbed into bed without undressing, pulled the covers over her head, and wished for the morning.

They both had late classes on Wednesdays, so it was almost ten o'clock before Carrie got up. She saw Jen sitting at their small table peeling an orange.

"Morning, Carrie. Want an orange? Some toast, maybe?"

Carrie didn't know how to react. Should she just pretend along with Jen that nothing strange had happened the night before? "Um, toast, please."

Jen put two pieces of bread in their toaster. "I suppose you're wondering about last night," she said. "I wish you could have been there at the start when I explained everything we were going to do."

"It was so strange, so …"

"So deep? So real? Carrie, what you almost experienced last

night was the beginning of the most beautiful thing in the world. The sacred feminine."

The toast popped up. Carrie, now out of bed, pulled the bread out of the toaster and began nibbling on a piece.

"What do the circle and the chanting have to do with the sacred feminine?"

Jen pushed her orange peel into a neat pile in the middle of the table. "The sacred feminine ritual can be done any number of ways. I thought this one best for those who may have experienced something similar in a church service before. That's what we were doing last night, you know. Having a worship service. Only we were worshiping the true god—male and female—in the form of the sacred feminine."

"The true god?" Carrie responded doubtfully.

"Yes. God is a divine essence that combines the fullness of all that is masculine and feminine, an essence that pervades all of life. The sacred feminine sees each person as inherently good, not starting in sin like Christians portray. We see our interdependence on nature, and we value our Divine Mother as the giver of birth to all. We see that magic is at work in our world, producing miracles we cannot explain. We value positive personal growth and self-esteem, realizing the value of each individual.

"We see the bad side of an individual not as inherent evil, but as the 'winter' of life, part of the cycle of learning. We value the cycles of life, including death. Death, just like life, is an individual choice. The sacred feminine celebrates death, whatever form it may take, as another step in the circle of life."

Jen's words had an almost hypnotic effect on Carrie. It took a few moments after Jen had ceased talking before Carrie found her own voice.

"So you have worship services for the sacred feminine?"

"Sometimes we do it that way," said Jen easily. "It helps introduce the concept to newcomers to the faith. But we each live out the sacred feminine in different ways. Some through communing with nature, some through sexual acts, some with enhancements."

"You mean drugs?"

"If that helps, it helps. But there is no one hard-and-fast way to experience the Goddess. You need to experiment, see what's best for you."

Jen picked up the orange peel and deposited it in the trash. "I gotta run to class. Catch you later."

Carrie fell back onto her bed. She thought about all Jen had just said. Then she thought of her talks with Evan. She couldn't get his words out of her head.

You must make your choice. Who do you say Jesus is?

She reached under her mattress for what she had hidden there. It had to still be there. She felt it, gave it a tug, then collapsed back onto the bed and opened the Book that Evan had left out for the group to take.

She never made it to class.

———※◆⬅———

"Well folks, as you all know, I'm here tonight to talk to you about the power of symbols" (9). As *The Da Vinci Code* begins, this is how Robert Langdon opens his lecture at the American University of Paris.

Well folks, we are likewise here at whatever hour you are reading our book, to *write* to you about the power of symbols. *The Da Vinci Code* employs powerful symbols to communicate its mysterious code. In fact, it is no accident that the very first chapter introduces a main character who is lecturing on *pagan* symbolism.

Leonardo da Vinci belonged to this arcane school of thought.

The lead characters are experts in such symbolism. Langdon is a Harvard professor of religious symbology and author of a book, *Symbols of the Lost Sacred Feminine*, which includes the iconography of goddess worship, fertility, Wicca, and Isis. Allegedly, Leonardo da Vinci belonged to this arcane school of thought (113), and was "an avid student of the occult."[1] Jacques Saunière, "knew more about pagan iconography than anyone else on earth" (77) and had "a passion for relics relating to fertility, goddess cults, Wicca, and the sacred feminine" (23).

At one level, the drama of the novel can be defined in the conflict of symbols it evokes. "In the battle between the pagan symbols and Christian symbols," says Langdon, "the pagans lost" (37). What the pagans lost is now resurrected by no less than Dan Brown himself. The battle is rejoined.

Is it true that the symbolism of the circle is simply innocent (343)?

Is it true that Baphomet is a harmless symbol for the goodness of sexuality and another way to speak of wisdom (316–321)?

Is it true that Satan is the result of "the Church's attempts to recast the horned fertility god as a symbol of evil" to demonize its opponents (316)?

Is it true that "the Church launched a smear campaign

against the pagan gods and goddesses, recasting their divine symbols as evil" (37)?

THE POWER OF THE CIRCLE

There is nothing simpler than a circle, except, perhaps, a straight line, but the circle contains a universe of meaning. *The Da Vinci Code* honors the sun (339) and speaks of "[t]he simplicity of the circle" (343), which is used in ritual worship (316).

But, one may argue, there's nothing mysterious and powerful about a simple circle!

If the circle is so common, so innocent, so powerless, why are pagan groups the world over in love with "the power of the circle"? In ancient Egyptian religion, the circle stood for the all-inclusiveness of the sun, one of the powers of Nature.[2] The early American non-Christian spiritualist, Ralph Waldo Emerson, even wrote a poem to "Circles," seeing himself and others as a unique planet with "no outside, no enclosing walls, no circumference to us."[3] From the center of such a limitless, circular universe the self reigns supreme.

As I (Peter) arrived in the ultramodern airport of Sydney, I noticed huge billboard-sized photos of well-known Australian athletes and personalities. One was titled *The Dreaming* and showed a dancing naked aborigine. "The Dreaming," I discovered, is the name for Australian aboriginal spirituality. What the aborigines call "dreaming" we call "altered states of consciousness." To achieve this state through ritual, the aboriginal celebrants dance in a circle and create "*the power of the circle ... a sacred site* [which] ... *concentrates and focuses energy* ... out of which an Ancestor [spirit] emerges."[4]

The circle is not copyrighted by Emerson and the aborigines. It is also the most important symbol in the Wicca religion, a spiritual tradition that worships Nature. In their basic ritual, Wiccans cast a "sacred circle" to capture the powers of the natural universe. "The circle is the sacred space created around an altar, either in a room or in a bush setting. It defines the area of ritual, holds within it the positive energy used for magick (sic), and wards off negative forces."[5]

"The power of the circle" is even taking on a political form. The Global Renaissance Alliance is a group of twenty-first-century, sophisticated, socially active people, many of whom are well-known promoters of the "New Spirituality." This group is determined to bring political change to America via a spirituality much like the one proposed in *The Da Vinci Code*. You can see on their web site that they construct their program on "the ancient archetypal symbol of a circle, ... calling forth [the] ... magic[al] energies that represent unity, harmony and wholeness."[6]

The circle is the most important symbol in Wicca, a spiritual tradition that worships Nature.

They think the power of the circle connects humanity to its "divine source," so humans can live on "a truly loving planet." The divine source is not the God of the Bible. It is Nature herself. They borrow from Wiccan language and believe that the circle makes the whole earth, indeed the entire universe, into "sacred ground."[7]

Maybe you think we're going a little overboard here. How seriously should we take such a group? In case you have any doubts of the pagan and religious nature of this "political" vision, here is the statement from the Global Renaissance Alliance:

> The circle process embodies an ancient wisdom,
> the feminine wisdom of Sophia and Mary,
> Demeter, Cybele and Isis; the earthy and mystical
> wisdom of our tribal ancestors and our indigenous
> peoples.[8]

Politics is going spiritual in ways we never imagined! Did you ever believe a candidate for the presidency of the United States would say he was running for office "to enable the Goddess of peace to encircle within her arms all the children of this country and all the children of the world"?[9] Prepare yourself for goddess geo-politics!

THE "DIVINE, MAGICAL" PENTAGRAM

Good mystery novels get going with the first dead body. So does *The Da Vinci Code*. Jacques Saunière's corpse on the floor of the Louvre is not just any old dead body. It forms da Vinci's *Vitruvian Man*, the five points within a circle, which is the pentagram.

The pentagram, Langdon tells his Harvard class, "is one of the most powerful images you will see ... [It] is considered both divine and magical by many cultures" (96). It is one of the pre-Christian symbols favored by *The Da Vinci Code*, going back "four thousand years before Christ" (35), and is, says Langdon, "[p]rimarily a pagan ... religious symbol" (35).

Indeed, the pentagram was important to almost every ancient culture, including those of Latin America, India, China, and Egypt. Archaeologists have found the pentagram scratched on the walls of Neolithic caves and in Babylonian drawings where it marks the pattern of the planet Venus as it journeys through the skies.[10] The pentagram is another favored symbol of Wiccans[11] and holds much symbolic meaning in Neo-Pagan ritual.[12] It has also been used as a magical or occult symbol by the Pythagoreans, Masons, Gnostics, Kabalists, magicians, and Satanists.[13]

> *Just as we associate Christianity with a cross and Judaism with the six-pointed star, pagans use the pentagram.*

Just as we associate Christianity with the cross and Judaism with the six-pointed star, pagans use the pentagram, a symbol of the magical rituals of pagan religions everywhere. It has never been used as a Christian symbol.[14]

It is surely significant that *The Da Vinci Code* dismisses the one obviously Christian symbol, the cross, as a symbol of violence and torture (145) and gives preference to a "peaceful cross ..." with four arms of equal length that "predated Christianity by fifteen hundred years" (145).

The circle that sometimes surrounds the pentagram represents "sacred space," typical of pagan religion. It is often used in pagan rituals as a focal point, as one Wiccan site proposes, to move "beyond the realms of physical form and our limited five senses, to explore the infinite possibilities that exist within the Universe."[15] This is one example of the spirituality described in the previous chapter.

The pentagram is sometimes seen with a goat's or ram's head within it, called Baphomet. Who is Baphomet?

BAPHOMET

In *The Da Vinci Code* Baphomet is a harmless "pagan god" (316), symbol of sexuality and an anagram for wisdom, or Sophia (318–321). He is not a symbol for Satan, since most pagans do not believe Satan exists.

Many accounts of the idol Baphomet come from the trials of the Templars, who were accused of "the worship of Baphomet."[16] Nineteenth-century writers believed that the Templars were devil-worshiping occultists[17] and saw in Baphomet the god of pleasure and the symbol of rebellion against the Christian church.[18] Baphomet, as the horned fertility god, is certainly pre-Christian. The most familiar image of Baphomet portrays him seated, as a winged, goat-headed and goat-footed man with a woman's breasts, a flame on his forehead, and a phallus at his groin.[19]

In the twentieth century, German occultists formed the secret *Ordo Templi Orientis* (Order of Templars in the East). As head of their British section, they installed

Most pagans do not believe Satan exists.

As Paul says, there is nothing in common between God and Satan.

the English occultist Aleister Crowley, who took Baphomet as his magical name. In the 1960s, Simon LaVey established the goat-headed Baphomet within a circle as the sign of the present Church of Satan.[20]

Whether used in the nature-worshiping Wiccan kind of spirituality or in the personalized Satanist kind, Baphomet is a symbol of paganism, which has nothing to do with the Bible. With regard to Satan in the main, Wiccans will not admit Satanists into their celebrations because they claim Satan is a creation of Christianity.[21] We find the same approach in *The Da Vinci Code*.

SATAN

Like some contemporary religious liberals, Brown finds no place in true spirituality for personal evil or a personal devil. He dismisses "[t]he modern belief in a horned devil known as Satan," as "the Church's attempts to recast the horned fertility god as a symbol of evil" (316).

Elaine Pagels, famous for her book on the Gnostic Gospels, wrote another book, *The Origin of Satan*,[22] which lends academic support to the Wiccan belief about Satan. Pagels argues that Satan, or the devil as an evil being, only emerged to prominence out of the New Testament and was used to affirm one group's beliefs while demonizing the group's opponents.

The approach Pagels and others take in order to undermine biblical faith goes further than the earlier liberals, who tried to *reinterpret* what the New Testament said. The modern approach claims that the entire New Testament is only one (wrong) take on Jesus. It opts for another "authentic" stream, dismissing the New Testament and rejecting the idea of divinely inspired truth. Its "truth" teaches that the world cannot be divided into the forces of good and the forces of evil.

Pagels places herself in a superior tradition in which she includes the Gnostics, Francis of Assisi, and Martin Luther King. She dismisses the words of Jesus, who said to those who opposed Him, "You are of your father, the devil" (John 8:44), and the words of Paul, who called those who preached another gospel "servants of Satan" (2 Corinthians 11:15).

The Da Vinci Code refuses to admit the existence of Satan, and in the same way says that the term *heretic* was created by the church in Constantine's time to demonize those who held to the religion contained in the Gnostic texts (234). *The Da Vinci Code* takes the same line as Pagels, who popularized the same Gnostic texts. The "Gnostic Empire" is striking back, using all the arrows in its quiver.

What if Pagels and *The Da Vinci Code* are wrong, duped by the "father of lies," who, as C. S. Lewis notes in the *Screwtape Letters*, loves humans to deny Satan's existence? We firmly believe what the New Testament teaches: There is real evil in the

Brown's admiration of pagan spirituality is best evidenced in the special place his book grants the Goddess.

universe, and it has a personal source. By making this statement, we are not demonizing people, but warning them that real demons can deceive and influence them. We didn't write the Bible. It is the Bible that reminds us that all human beings are made in the image of God, and we cannot escape the cosmic struggle between right and wrong. Evil is a mystery, but it is not another face of God, the good Creator. As Paul says, there is nothing in common between Christ and Satan (2 Corinthians 6:15). Good and evil cannot mix. Good and evil cannot be rolled into one happy, inclusive circle. In fact, Christians believe that evil is the exclusion—the separation from good—from God.

THE GODDESS

The inclusive circle is most clearly expressed in the symbol of the Goddess or the "sacred feminine" (238). The proof? The secret society, whose mission is to preserve the "real" truth of Christianity, is not Christian at all. As the book says, the Priory of Sion is "*the* pagan goddess worship cult" (113). The Priory's goal is to undo the evil perpetrated by "Constantine and his male successors" in the church, who "demonized the sacred feminine, obliterating the goddess from modern religion forever" (124).

Goddess in the Past

While claiming to be calmly objective and inclusive, *The Da Vinci Code* accuses the church of "launch[ing] a smear campaign against the pagan gods and goddesses, recasting their divine symbols as evil" (37). Nobody seems to have a corner on "smearing," for *The Da Vinci Code*'s attack on the church simply fails to discuss the theological reasons for Christianity's refusal of paganism. At the same time, the novel betrays its own deeply religious commitments to a "pre-Christian" (36) pagan spirituality (specifically, "the pentacle's true origins"), which it finds "actually quite godly" and its symbols "divine" (37).

The author's admiration for pagan spirituality is best evidenced in the special place his book grants the Goddess. This is no innocent choice, for the Goddess represents one of the most powerful paganizing forces in modern society. Many radical feminists have also gone "pre-Christian," arguing, as one of them does, that spiritual progress means embracing "the Neolithic, pagan, matriarchal perception of the sacred universe itself."[23]

The Goddess certainly is pre-Christian. She emerges from the mists of time, out of the East, as the savior from death. The Egyptian Isis, the goddess of witchcraft and magic, goes back to around 3000 B.C.[24] The pagan religion of ancient Ugarit (around 2500 B.C.) worshiped the goddess Anat, who restored Baal to life.[25] The goddess Istar, a spiritual force around 1800 B.C. in ancient Babylon, supposedly bridged the gap between the living and the dead with her secret power.[26] In ancient Canaan, the goddess Asherah, resembling Istar and Anat, was the consort of Baal.[27] The Syrian goddess Cybele or Atargatis had all the qualities of Anat.[28] Often known as the Great Mother, the Goddess under many names communicated the powers of death in the unseen spirit world. The ancient Goddess is on a roll these days.

Goddess in the Present

You may think American religion is in crisis. Not so, according to some. It is only in transformation. *When God Becomes Goddess*, a recent book of "Christian" theology, argues that "certain elements of traditional religious belief and practice [i.e., Christianity] are passing away and a new kind of religiosity is poised to take its place."[29] The religiosity that is ready to take its place is that of the Goddess.

The Goddess has also entered the popular mainstream through witchcraft. Hollywood has recently produced a series of movies that takes us into bewitched territory: *The Blair Witch Project*, *The Craft* (showing teen practitioners), *The Crucible*; while television has given us ABC's *Sabrina: the Teenage Witch*, and WB's *Charmed*. Hot Topic, an in-your-face clothes store for teenagers in our local mall, includes a rack of books on popular witchcraft. Jennifer Hunter's *21st Century Wicca: A Young Witch's Guide to the Magical Life* is a best-seller. Officially sanctioned Wiccan services now take place on army bases and in prisons throughout the land, and witch clergy perform marriages with the formal blessing of the New York City Council.

Such approval of pagan practice is not unique to the United States. Denmark has announced it will allow a group that worships Thor, Odin, and other Norse gods to conduct legal marriages. "It would be wrong if the indigenous religion of this country wasn't recognized," said Tove Fergo, a Lutheran minister and government Minister for Ecclesiastic Affairs.[30]

Jean Houston was a friend and counselor of First Lady Hillary Clinton during the 1990s. Houston believes our society needs to be rebuilt through the myth of the goddess Isis and her consort Osiris.[31] Our leaders are promoting the Goddess of Magic and the Underworld as the savior who can bring us social, cultural, and spiritual transformation. They reason that the Gnostic "Christians" wor- shiped the mysteries of Isis, the Great Mother,[32] so as their texts are reread and trusted, their gods are revived. The title of a book written a few years ago expresses *The Da Vinci Code*'s deep message: *The Once and Future Goddess: A Symbol for Our Time.*[33] The old Goddess has come over the seas of time and landed on our shores with plans to transform us!

The sacred feminine assures us that everything in Nature, including our inner self, is divine.

The "sacred feminine" really means the reign of Mother Nature. Nature and its forces determine everything. The sacred feminine assures us that everything in Nature, including our inner self, is divine. A modern witch called Miriam Starhawk defines the Goddess:

> She is the great forces of birth, growth, death, and regeneration that move through the universe. Her many aspects are the faces we put on these forces so we can interact with them. She is immanent within us as well as in nature.[34]

Joseph Campbell, who was a guru to George Lucas, director of *Star Wars*, said, "In religions where the god or creator is the mother, the world is her body. There is nowhere else."[35] Campbell was not an atheist, as you can see. He was plenty spiritual. But his spirituality was pagan. *God* is a word he used to mean the divinity of all natural things. He didn't use the word to mean a God who is outside creation and who is in fact its origin. Campbell's god was a kind of impersonal presence, to be found everywhere, in everything.[36]

THE SPIRITUALITY OF THE GODDESS

Those who see Nature this way are taking part in a dark, magical kind of spirituality. A scholar who studied Isis explains that her magic is "real wisdom," since it gives insight into the mystery of life and death.[37] When people take part in initiation rites into her mysteries and in the ecstatic secret experiences of her temples, they get a foretaste of immortality.[38] The experiences described in Goddess worship are life-changing "conversion" experiences. They are trance-like ecstatic highs provoked by drugs,[39] dance, music,[40] flogging,[41] and other techniques. They allow the believer to escape the fear of death, and they claim to allow escape from death itself.

Here is one of the few first-person accounts we have of someone who, in the second century A.D., went through the initiation rites of the mysteries of Isis:

> I approached the frontier of death, I set foot on the
> threshold of the underworld; I journeyed through
> all the elements and came back, I saw the sun at

midnight, sparkling in white light; I came close to
the gods of the upper and the nether world and
adored them from near at hand.[42]

In the initiation to the Goddess, there is that same experience of opposites: life and death, night and day, darkness and
light.[43] The new disciple sees himself as Osiris, the husband
of Isis, whom she brings back from the dead. So life and
death are joined, and death is overcome. This mystical, mind-
blowing experience is typical of paganism, because it tries to
join the opposites.[44] *The Da Vinci Code* claims that the worship
of Isis included sex rites (308). Knowing the Gnostics, this is
possible, even probable. However, reports from that era are
few and guarded.

The modern description of Goddess worship is more like
what we find in *The Da Vinci Code*. Miriam Starhawk, who is a
very well-known and best-selling witch, describes her belief
as the worship of two deities: the Mother Goddess, who
brings life into existence, and the Horned God, a male hunter
who died and was resurrected each year. This is the same
basic story that we find in the paganism going back to 3000
B.C. Worshipers include both male priests (dressed in skins
and horns in identification with the god and the herds [an
obvious form of Baphomet]), but it is naked priestesses who
preside, embodying the fertility of the Goddess. When priestesses are naked, sex rites—as *The Da Vinci Code* describes
them—are not far away, especially since the Goddess (and
doubtless, her priestesses) gives birth to the Divine Child,
who is her consort, son, and seed.[45]

THE GODDESS COMES TO AMERICA

The symbol of the Goddess and the spirituality it produces find no place in biblical faith. Nevertheless, the publishing arm of a mainline Christian denomination commends to the faithful the work of a theologian/pagan priestess, and says of her book, *Celebrating Her*,

> Deep within the womb of the earth lies a memory of
> a sacredness nearly buried under the weight of
> patriarchy. … More and more women—especially
> those with Christian backgrounds—are being drawn
> to this empowering, goddess-centered worship.[46]

Readers of *our* book are warned that the Goddess will not lead them into Christian worship, as Sue Monk Kidd's book joyfully affirms, but right out of it. Her title says it all: *The Dance of the Dissident Daughter: A Woman's Journey from Christian Tradition to the Sacred Feminine.*[47] This is at the core of what the sacred feminine means!

In our own backyard, San Diego, there is a project to welcome all those who make the exit. A group of Goddess worshipers plans to build a temple to the Goddess called the Center of the Divine Feminine. Amenities will include a five-hundred-person worship hall, a large flat area for circle ceremonies, fountains, statuary, a maypole, a peace pole, prayer flags, a fire pit, labyrinths, hot baths, natural water ponds, and herb and vegetable gardens.[48] The Temple of Diana/Artemis (a form of Isis), one of the wonders of the ancient world that dominated the city of Ephesus at the time of Paul, immediately jumps to mind. This is no longer fiction. For, as this pagan movement gains financial clout and institutional visibility, we are surely seeing only the beginning of the power of the sacred feminine.

An ex-Roman Catholic theologian with two doctorates, Mary Daly, who now calls herself an eco-feminist lesbian witch, welcomes this journey out from Christianity as "the Second Coming of the Goddess." She declares, in sobering terms,

> The antichrist and the Second Coming are synony-
> mous. This Second Coming is not the return of
> Christ but a new arrival of female presence. ... The
> Second Coming, then, means that the prophetic
> dimension in the symbol of the great Goddess ... is
> the key to salvation from servitude.[49]

Symbols are very important to us. We look to symbols as a type of road map to lead us along the way, and the symbols we choose to heed can determine our quality of life here—and in the hereafter.

So again, we are faced with a choice, in this case between symbols—the cross of Christ or the symbols of paganism (Wicca, witchcraft, the sacred feminine, Baphomet, and the Goddess). The question before us is, which version of history and faith with all of its accompanying symbols is true, and which is a lie?

But that question itself has a Christian bias, doesn't it? Because from a pagan view of the world, the truth and the lie would also simply be encircled as one and the same—like life and death, good and evil, truth and lie become one. Echoing

MONA LISA

In Italian, she is known as La Gioconda, "The Merry One." The name may also be a clue as to the subject of the world's most famous portrait. Mona Lisa Gherardini dle Gioconda of Florentine is the most often mentioned model for the *Mona Lisa*. Other possibilities include da Vinci's mother, Caterina, and da Vinci himself in drag. The latter suggestion is dismissed by almost all reputable art historians.

What is known is that it is in the *Mona Lisa* that da Vinci perfected his technique of sfumato, a method of creating a perception of haze covering the painting. It is this trick of light, as well as the imperceptible smile on the *Mona Lisa*'s face, that causes one to see a new picture every time it is viewed.

the words of Pilate as he sent Jesus to the cross, the pagan has to ask, "What is truth?"(John 18:38) … and in the same breath, is there such a thing as a lie? But we all know there is such thing as a lie, don't we? We know bigotry is a lie; we know that dehumanizing women as sex objects is a lie. And what of the Gnostic and pagan claim that the biblical Gospels are lies? If we're willing to call something false, there must also be a choice of truth.

The Jesus of the Christian New Testament isn't in the least confused on the matter. He unabashedly calls Himself the sole source of truth—in fact, He literally declares that He Himself *is* "the truth" (as well as the "life," and the only "way" to God, as recorded by that firsthand witness, John [14:6]). But to the pagan way of thinking and believing, should it really matter to us if Jesus was lying—if truth and lies are all in the circle of oneness? It's a question that should give all thinking seekers great cause for concern, especially if the premise of their pursuit is that it doesn't matter if they are following a lie. After all, what's the difference between truth and lie?

Now with the question of "is there such a thing as truth" before us, let's consider the question of why we should care about all of this symbolism. To the authentic Christian's way of thinking, symbolism has an ironic potential for being a profound distraction *from* truth. (Admittedly, that's because we believe there *is* such a thing as an absolute, knowable truth.) And just as idolatry amounts to worshiping the created instead of the Creator (the tree, rather than the Maker of the tree), so symbols can become our obsessive focus of devotion. In fact, the symbol can block our view of the truth to which it is supposed to be pointing.

Christians do not claim to worship the cross, but rather they worship God the Son who hung on the cross. They do not claim to worship an empty tomb, but rather the Christ who rose from the tomb. Symbols can be a great help for our understanding. But what (or better, who) is it that we are trying to understand?

It all comes full circle (as it were) back to the central question: Is the Jesus of the Christian Gospels who He says He is? Is He really God, or is He simply a distraction? Is the Jesus of the Bible the truth ... or a lie?

The "symbol of the great Goddess," like all the other "pre-Christian" pagan symbols esteemed by The Da Vinci Code *that we have examined in this chapter, erases one more huge piece of the Divine Arc.*

CHAPTER 10

At the level of the plot, heroes track down the Holy Grail, outsmarting adversaries and overcoming resistance from all directions.

At the level of the code, a deep subplot—the "sacred feminine"—heroically emerges from the shadows of the past. Against all odds, this philosophical heroine will undo the male power of the institutional church and banish to the cultural margins "third-century [Christianity, its views on women, and its] laws" that are "not workable in today's society" (416).

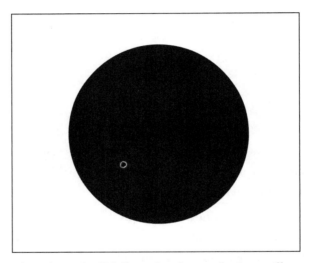

Thus the code, if followed to its conclusion, will exclude the Divine Arc completely, and leave you on your own.

CRACKING THE CODE

You gonna have to serve somebody. It may be the devil or it may be the Lord.
Bob Dylan, Gotta Serve Somebody

"Evan, this is Carrie. Can we talk?" It was dinnertime. Carrie had been reading the Bible all day, starting right at the beginning of the New Testament.

"Sure, Carrie. What's on your mind?"

"Well, can we meet somewhere? I need to talk with you face-to-face."

"I'm going to church in about an hour. Do you want to meet now or after I get back?"

"Now!" Carrie was surprised at her response. "Now, if it's okay. I won't hold you up—I promise."

They met at Café Bona and sat at the same table they had occupied just a few weeks before. "You're wearing jeans! I thought you were going to church," Carrie blurted.

"You don't need to wear a suit to teach Sunday school," Evan responded. Then he looked sideways at her and added, "You're looking pretty casual yourself."

Carrie blushed. She had run a brush through her hair but hadn't bothered with any makeup. "I didn't have time to get ready. This is too important." Carrie quickly went on to explain what she had seen the night before. When she finished, she felt completely drained. "What I don't understand is why I feel the way I do today," she concluded.

"You mean confused?" asked Evan.

"No, not really. I'm very clear about how I feel about the ritual last night. What I'm feeling today is, well, more a sense of emptiness."

Evan nodded gently. He reached into his ever-present backpack and pulled out a blank piece of paper. In the middle he drew a circle.

"You say your roommate said the sacred feminine represents itself as a circle?"

"Yes," replied Carrie. "She says the circle is whole and complete, encompassing everything within."

"Well, she's partly right. There is a circle that is whole and complete, and it does encompass all of creation. But this paper isn't big enough to draw it."

"I don't get what you're saying," said Carrie.

"Okay—let's say this circle is us—or let's say it's you. How do you feel about controlling all of creation? Or even just controlling your immediate surroundings? Can you get your arms around all the problems just in this coffee shop?"

Carrie shook her head.

"Yet, that is just what Jen is trying to have you do, Carrie. She thinks we can be this lone circle, the center of our universe. By calling herself her own goddess, she thinks no one will control her or tell her what to do."

"Evan," said Carrie, "every person should be the center of her own universe. Everyone should be free to choose what to believe and how to act on that belief. That is a central right given to us as individuals. I'm not willing to allow anyone else into my 'circle,' as you put it."

"What about evil, Carrie?" Evan responded. "If you allow all people to do whatever they want, then how do you deal with evil? If each circle is independent and unaccountable, then Hitler was not evil when he slaughtered millions of Jews. He was just acting on his own beliefs."

Carrie sat silent, not knowing how to respond.

"And if your circle is on its own, unaccountable to anyone, who can you ever turn to if you need help?"

"I don't need help—"

"Ah," interrupted Evan. "Think about that for a little while. I have to run, but I'll call you tonight. Okay?"

"How about I just come with you?" Carrie asked, surprising both of them. "I mean, if that's okay."

Evan stood up. "That's more than okay. It's great!"

———◆———

The stone towers and green copper roof of the Church of Saint-Sulpice stand out against the dull gray of the Parisian skyline. In this church, *The Da Vinci Code* sets the brutal murder of Sister Sandrine by Silas, an albino monk. In passing, the story mentions that the church was built over the ruins of a temple to Isis (88) and contains a colossal pyramid-shaped obelisk, which, in Egyptian religion, symbolized the rays of the sun (104). In this seemingly minor detail, we begin to see the "code."

The drama of the novel occurs on two levels.

At the level of the plot, heroes track down the Holy Grail, outsmarting adversaries and overcoming resistance from all directions.

At the level of the code, a deep subplot—the "sacred feminine"—heroically emerges from the shadows of the past. Against all odds, this philosophical heroine will undo the male power of the institutional church and banish to the cultural margins "third-century [Christianity, its views on women, and its] laws" that are "not workable in today's society" (416).

THE "NEW AGE" OF AQUARIUS

The Saint-Sulpice church, an impressive icon of Christianity, proudly occupies the modern public square. But the novel uncovers the irony of the church's real foundations: Goddess-worshiping paganism. Those foundations, suppressed for centuries, are rising again to displace the pretender and to reclaim their rightful place. The old, earlier, and authentic spirituality is replacing the later imposter. Pre-Christian peace-loving "matriarchal paganism" and the "sacred feminine" will overcome violent "patriarchal Christianity" and the faith of our power-hungry macho church fathers (124). In short, the pre-Christian Goddess will replace the God of the Bible.

In the Age of Aquarius, the pre-Christian Goddess will replace the God of the Bible.

For many in our culture, the new "gospel" announced by *The Da Vinci Code* is good news. The Age of Aquarius replaces the Age of Pisces (401). "The Vatican faces a crisis of faith unprecedented in its two-millennia history," which also marks the end of "the two-thousand-year-long astrological Age of Pisces—the fish, which is also the sign of Jesus" (267). The Priory of Sion has been "waiting for the right moment in history to share their secret. A time when the world is ready to handle the truth" (295), [a time when] "we are entering the Age of Aquarius—the water bearer—whose ideals claim that man will learn the *truth* and be able to think for himself" (268).

Since the 1960s, modern mystics have hailed this "New Age" of Aquarius as the return of pagan spirituality. They call the Age of Pisces the "Christian interlude"—a parenthesis between two eras of paganism. Since the sixties, American history has witnessed a revolution far more powerful than the one that established this country as an independent nation. The recent revolutionaries have cut us free from our Christian-inspired past. In one generation, they have established new and radical views of the family, education, morals, marriage, sexuality, spirituality, and God. Their views have become the new politically correct orthodoxy. The bard of the cultural revolution, Bob Dylan, sang,

> Come mothers and fathers throughout the land
> and don't criticize what you can't understand,
> your sons and your daughters are beyond your
> command.
> > Your old road is rapidly agin' ...
> for the loser now will be later to win,
> for the times they are a-changin'. [1]

At the risk of ourselves sounding as if we're ringing the alarms of vast conspiracies, it's hard not to see a connection between the supposedly passé movement of the sixties generation and the neo-paganism of today. The times have changed, and the new influencers, including Dan Brown, are rewriting history. Furthermore, it's simply naïve to dismiss the significant influence that this worldview is having on the media, education, and politics. Beliefs do impact how we live and the choices we make.

For nearly a generation, radical feminists have recommended "a new view of reality." In some churches, preachers speak of a Jesus whose body rotted in the grave. This new thinking will bring about "a new science and spirituality," a "new politics and economics, where the old nation state ... will wither away." All this will come about, in particular "through the reaffirmation and celebration of the transformative mysteries symbolized by the Chalice."[2]

According to *The Da Vinci Code*, this age "has arrived" as "the End of Days" (268). Marie, Jacques Saunière's "wife," declares with the conviction of a believer, "We are beginning to sense the need to restore the sacred feminine," and exhorts Langdon with the passion of a missionary: "Sing her song. The world needs modern troubadours" (444).

Toward Global Religious Unity

Another church building makes the point clearer. Langdon hears the call to action as he gazes up at Rosslyn Chapel, a church supposedly built by the Templars who, according to one of the novel's well-crafted sayings, "had left no stone uncarved" (434). In this chapel, known as "the Cathedral of Codes," everything comes together (432). In this chapel the Isis foundations, so hidden at the Saint-Sulpice church, are exposed in all their glory. The carvings are the code.

> Each block [of the chapel] was carved with a symbol ... to form a bizarre multifaceted surface (436). ... Christian cruciforms, Jewish stars, Masonic seals, Templar crosses, cornucopias, pyramids, astrological signs, plants, vegetables, pentacles, and roses ... Rosslyn Chapel was a shrine to all faiths ... to all traditions ... and, above all, to nature and the goddess (434).

The code stands for the unity of all faiths, founded on the worship of Nature and the Goddess. This global faith will include a new pope and a church that follows him into pagan unity—the blending of opposing religions and philosophies into one, or syncretism (415–416).

Such an idea is far from novel. A second-century A.D. visitor to Apollo's temple at Didyma (in present-day Turkey) described it as a "circle of altars to every god."[3] One pagan priest of the period described himself as a "priest of all the gods."[4]

This global faith will include a new pope and a church that follows him into pagan syncretism.

The vision of global religious unity drives many spiritual people in our time. As one modern Isis priestess put it, "It may be that Sophia/Isis is about to be ... a beacon to Christians, Jews, Gnostics and Pagans alike."[5]

Isis will bring religious unity on her pagan terms, this time on a planetary scale. If such a synthesis can be pulled off in

It is at this deep

spiritual level

that this book's

attack on

Christianity

is the most

vicious.

America, says a United Methodist lesbian professor at Harvard, it would be "the greatest form of lasting leadership we [could] offer the world."[6] America's new religious calling is to develop a unified spirituality that will save the planet. For this new calling, we will also need a new Jesus.

Recalling an earlier quote in *American Jesus: How the Son of God Became a National Icon,*[7] the author argues that "Jesus won't become a national figure unless he can move outside Christianity." A non-Christian Jesus? Such was the Jesus of the Gnostic texts, and such is the Jesus of *The Da Vinci Code.*

In our fractured world of autonomous, unconnected people, the Goddess brings good news. It is claimed she will put our world together again. She will unite ecological wisdom, economic justice, human rights, women's liberation, equality and harmony between the sexes, pan-sexual freedom, personal significance, global peace, religious unity, utopian dreams, life on our own terms, and deep spirituality.

AN IDEOLOGICAL CALL TO ARMS

This ideology is what the *The Da Vinci Code* believes and teaches in story form. The book is written from a particular religious ideology. It is not a neutral fictional tale that adds a few historical facts for a ring of truth. It is a propaganda piece for a religious worldview. And that's fair enough, because it could be said that authors' worldviews impact any work of fiction. But readers of Brown's novel need to realize that his commitment to Neo-Pagan religious assumptions also color his choice of "facts" and everything he affirms through his characters.

It is at this deep spiritual level that the book's attack on Christianity is the most vicious. We must, of course, answer its digs at the Bible and the authentic Jesus. However, the real significance of the book is its clear intention to undermine the very foundation of biblical faith and to establish in its place an opposing religious system. Because Brown has adopted the pagan worldview, he is not content to shoot a few BBs at the facts of church history. He wants to blow a hole in the foundations of the worldview of the Bible.

Under the guise of a novel, *The Da Vinci Code* is an ideological call to arms. During wartime, codes are useful for communicating crucial messages in hidden ways. As much as we wish we could ignore it, there is a *spiritual* war for the human soul. Two views of religion are warring in our day, and simply pretending otherwise won't make it go away. There might be hundreds of factions (religions) with their unique little agendas, but ultimately they all will eventually align themselves under two fundamental alliances: pagan monism and biblical theism.

Ultimately, there are not hundreds of religions. There are two.

Pagan Monism ...

The religious worldview of *The Da Vinci Code* celebrates the soft, inclusive womb of the Goddess, from which everything emerges and to which it all returns. In this vision, the universe is one, so it can be called monism (think "one-ism"). Remember the circle at the end of chapter 9? According to monism, everything is in that circle—the divine, the human, animals, rocks, trees. Everything, according to this worldview, shares the same nature. There is no other circle, no other reality. In the divine union of Nature and humanity, everything is possible. When we understand this "all is one" mentality, we can better understand *The Da Vinci Code*'s *Hieros Gamos* or "sacred marriage." The book's heroes come to grips with this shocking group-sex rite because it represents an ultimate spiritual experience—one shared, it is claimed, by all religions. It is known under several names: the *unio mystica*—the "mystical union," "deification" (becoming divine), "the seventh, highest mansion," "holy marriage," or "unitive vision."[8]

But with all of her diverse representations and forms, it is important to understand that the Goddess is only a symbol. She personifies the divine mystery in all things. Her ladyship exists only to express the fact that there is no personal deity. The "divine feminine" is an impersonal "force" that animates everything.

... vs. Biblical Theism

There is one worldview that cannot fit into the soft circle of the pagans: *theism,* the time-tested worldview of the Bible. It cannot fit into the pagan, monistic circle because it honors God as Lord and Creator—as being outside the circle. In order to express the mystery of this transcendent God, the God who is beyond His created order, we draw an arc. It is placed above the circle in the same way God is above 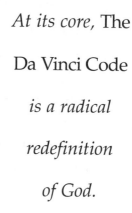 His creation. God and the universe are distinct, as distinct as a painter from his painting, as distinct as da Vinci from his *Last Supper*.

At its core, The Da Vinci Code *is a radical redefinition of God.*

C. S. Lewis wrote, "God is a particular Thing."[9] God is not some kind of energy contained in the monistic circle, or "the circle of life." He is outside it, the Divine Arc appearing above the circle of creation. In contrast to the increasingly popular notion of the circle of life, the Bible reveals a very different view of God. The prophet Isaiah, in the eighth century B.C., said of Jahweh, "He sits enthroned above the circle of the earth" (Isaiah 40:22). God has His own place, His own domain of existence. No created circle of life can contain Him.

That is what we mean when we say that God is holy. "Holy" means "set apart" for a special place or function. God has a special place as Creator distinct from our place as creatures. We honor this understanding of God when we pray to "Our Father in heaven" (Matthew 6:9). That Father is the source of our personhood and the designer of our intricate universe. C. S. Lewis also wrote that the pagan god who is everything (and thus, in a sense, nothing) appears as a "mere zero," a "nonentity," a "featureless generality."[10]

Behind the debates and conflicting facts, at its core *The Da*

Vinci Code is a radical redefinition of God as the impersonal force of nature.

NOTHING HAS CHANGED

The Da Vinci Code is a reader-friendly, airbrushed version of a spirituality that denies the essence of biblical faith and, in particular, the biblical revelation of God. *This spirituality is not a version of Christianity*, as contemporary skeptics claim by appealing to the early Gnostics. It is instead a denial of all that Christianity holds dear.

In a sense, nothing has changed. In the ancient world, there were two kinds of Gnostics: those with no relationship to Christianity, and those who tried to pass themselves off as Christians. In the early centuries of the church, Christian leaders went through the same process we have presented in this book. They consistently showed that Gnosticism was a religion different from true Christianity.

After two thousand years, the conflict over spiritual truth remains.

Tertullian, a Christian historian of those early days, spoke of the Gnostics' "blasphemy against the Creator,"[11] saying "they make no distinction between pagans and believers in their churches."[12] He charged that "they have commerce with magicians, [peddlers], astrologers and philosophers."[13] A modern Gnostic, claiming no attachment to the faith of the Bible, describes the old "Christian" Gnostics the way the early church fathers did. He maintains that Gnosticism in the early church kept the Christian wording, but "its spirit is that of the latest paganism of the West."[14]

Paganism, whether ancient or modern, stands in opposition to the Christian message of the Bible. The new manifestation of paganism is forcing Christians to go through the same process of examining their faith as the early Christians did when the secret scrolls of the ancient Gnostics were first written.

Old Battle, New Culture

In the first three centuries of the church, Christians fought on two fronts. On the outside, they were persecuted by the pagan authorities of imperial Rome who forced them to confess "Caesar is Lord." On the inside, they had to withstand the Gnostic wolf in sheep's clothing who claimed to be Christian but adopted the pagan spirituality of the Roman Empire. We are now seeing a repeat of this two-front battle.

As our culture becomes a more decadent Rome,[15] our struggle for truth resembles that of the early church as we, too, face those who call themselves believers in Christ but are really Gnostics. After two thousand years, the conflict over spiritual truth remains.

The Da Vinci Code implies that the conflict is between objective historians and honest truth-seekers on one hand, and a closed-minded, intrusive church on the other. The fact is, we all find ourselves in a struggle for ultimate truth, fought with religious zeal on both sides.

Gods and Goddesses, or God?

The Da Vinci Code's spirituality shows up early in human history. The opening declaration of the Bible—"In the beginning God created the heavens and the earth" (Genesis 1:1)—is announced into a social context of Egyptian paganism; in particular, that of the worship of Isis, goddess of magic and the underworld. That same truth of God the transcendent Creator is repeated as Israel enters Canaan where Baal and Asherah, the god and goddess of fertility, were worshiped as the forces of divine nature.

In the ninth century B.C., Elijah called Israel to forsake these gods in order to serve the true and living God (1 Kings 17–19). In the eighth century B.C., the prophet Isaiah constantly contrasted the God of creation and redemption with the gods of Babylonian paganism (Isaiah 40–49). But the people were stubborn. Through the Bible comes a constant refrain that Israel had joined herself to Baal with disastrous consequences.

This is a history of conflict between two different religions vying for people's souls. Biblical religion and paganism are mutually exclusive. The Bible's claim to uniqueness is not motivated by narrow-mindedness, intolerance, or fear. It is unique in its radically different definition of God.

When we get to the New Testament, we see that Jesus, the founder of Christianity, built on the Old Testament. He warned about praying like the pagans (Matthew 6:7) and spoke of only two ways: the kingdom of God or the kingdom of Satan (Matthew 12:25–28). He reminded His audience that no one could know the Father without coming through Him, the Son.

The New Testament is full of black-and-white contrasts. Paul, one of Jesus' apostles, set in contrast two opposing systems:

The truth	The lie
Righteousness	Wickedness
Light	Darkness
Christ	Belial
The believer	The unbeliever
The temple of the living God	The temple of idols
The cup of the Lord	The cup of demons
The table of the Lord	The table of demons
The good teaching	The teaching of demons
Worship of the Creator	Worship of the creature
The glory of the immortal God	Images of mortal man
The wisdom of God	The wisdom of the world
No God but one	Many so-called gods
One Lord Jesus Christ	Many "lords"

Jesus and Paul were not inclusive of other pagan religions. There really is a difference between Gnosticism and Christianity.

THE CHOICE

After his conversion to Christianity, Bob Dylan sang in another song, "You gonna have to serve somebody, ... it may be the devil or it may be the Lord."[16] *The Da Vinci Code* and the book you are now reading show the choice everyone has to make. It is the same choice Elijah put before God's people: "How long will you waver between two opinions? If the LORD is God, follow him" (1 Kings 18:21).

There are only two religious paths, only two ways we can relate to the divine. Is God just Nature or is He the Creator of Nature? Your answer to that question changes everything you think and do. You are religious whether you realize it or not. Everyone worships and serves something. Either you will worship and serve "the creation," or you will worship and serve "the Creator—who is forever praised" (Romans 1:25). Either there is one circle, or there is a circle connected to an overriding arc.

WHICH GOOD NEWS?

Paganism and Christianity both offer good news. Both propose redemption. Paganism proposes *liberation from* the Creator to do one's own thing and to figure out how to save oneself. The Bible proposes *reconciliation with* the Creator, who comes to His creation as Savior. No one who truly seeks *that* Savior will be turned away.

The circle representing all of creation and the arc representing God who is above and beyond His creation are separate in two ways. First, we human creatures and God (the divine Creator) are different by nature. For instance, God has no beginning. We do. God knows everything. We don't. And there are many other differences.

Secondly, the Divine Arc and the created circle are separated by something else. In our most honest moments, moments when we are alone, every one of us knows that something within us in broken. It needs to be fixed. We even have a sense that we do not measure up. It might even be described as a sense of moral inferiority. Sometimes it is called guilt. We don't like to admit this to anyone, but it is true of all of us. The reason we feel as though something is broken is because something *is* broken. The reason we feel guilty is because we *are* guilty.

The God Who Came to Us

All of us were made for the purpose of enjoying a wonderful relationship with the Creator God Himself. But something devastated that relationship. It is called sin. As a result, a gap exists between us, as the created, and God the Creator. Every honest human feels this sense of estrangement, of loss, but it is not merely something felt. It is very real. And it's that state of separation—the "great divorce," as C. S. Lewis calls it—that is the essence of sin, much more so than the actions we've done. The "sins" that we commit and for which we feel more or less guilt are the symptoms of the real problem—being separated from God. *That* was the original sin of Eden, where the gap was introduced—where we first became our own gods (Genesis 3:4).

Furthermore, we can't close the gap. We can't fix the brokenness. We can't get to Him. So He must come to us. Only God can fix it. And God did fix it. He actually brought the arc (Himself) and the circle (us) together. He connected them. How? God decided to become "downwardly socially mobile" and take on human flesh. To become like us. And that is what He did, when God came in human form, in Jesus.

But there's more.

For a perfect and holy God to be bridged to something broken and sinful, the sinful one needs to be changed. So Jesus, who never sinned, took upon Himself the responsibility for our sin. We were then declared, in the legal jurisprudence of the universe, to be free of our sins. Not guilty! Romans 8:1 insists, "There is now no condemnation for those who are in Christ Jesus."

"And we know

that this man

really is

the Savior

of the world."

(John 4:42)

Those who will accept the gift are simply no longer responsible for their sin—their gap. What really makes us no longer responsible for our broken and sinful condition? What activates this reality? It is activated when we acknowledge the truth of it—that there is a gap of sin, and we want nothing more of it. We repent of it—we cross over and leave it behind.

Then the arc and the circle come together. We feel the passionate and loving arms of God wrapped around us. Then the sense of estrangement and loss leave. Jesus said, "I have come that they might have life, and have it to the full" (John 10:10). That's what happens when we are connected back to God!

This incredible truth about Jesus makes sense of Teabing's remark that "Jesus Christ was a historical figure of staggering influence, perhaps the most enigmatic and inspirational leader the world has ever seen" (231). A sex ritual with Mary Magdalene that produces a child hardly explains the influence of Jesus. Only a redeeming act of God with cosmic proportions can explain the impact of Jesus on the world. Only the biblical witness finally makes sense of Teabing's admission: Jesus is *the Savior of the world* (John 4:42).

Intimate Communion, True Joy

Our book does not intend to whitewash the obvious faults and misdeeds of those in the past who misrepresented Christ's church on earth. (Indeed, we join with any authentic Christian today in acknowledging our own faults and failures—the gap has been bridged, but God's changing our circles is the work of a lifetime … literally, our lifetime on earth.) Our book is also not an attempt to recover some lost "golden age" of the past. Its purpose has been, through a critical response to a major popular literary achievement, to clarify the two timeless religious options before which every human being must stand.

It is our firm belief and personal experience that there is comfort in the fact of an outside God to whom we can turn, who has promised not to turn us away if we seek Him. There is a real Redeemer who offers real forgiveness and deals definitively with our nagging guilt. We can relax in the control God has over the world. We have the possibility of truly forgiving others. We can have intimate communion with Him and joy in serving Him. We can find our place in the world!

As the authors of this book, it is our hope and prayer that God, the unique Creator and Savior, will use these pages to draw those wandering Teabings of the world who have recognized the greatness of Jesus, that they may find the true Holy Grail of the Gospel: Jesus Himself, the true Savior of the world.

Thus the code, if followed to its conclusion, will exclude the Divine Arc completely, and leave you on your own.

EPILOGUE

The Cross is greater than the code, and connects
our circle with the Divine Arc

CARRIE'S CHOICE

Jen was not in their room when Carrie returned. She was glad, for she needed to be alone.

On the wall hung the poster Jen had put up the night before. A large circle was drawn in the middle of the paper. Carrie sat in her chair looking at the circle. The words she had heard just hours before continued to echo in her mind.

"Jesus," said Jim Howard, pastor of the church Evan attended, "used the wood of the cross that he was nailed on to build a bridge."

Carrie had followed Evan into the church and sat in the back row. Evan had gone off to teach his children's class, but Carrie was not there to be with Evan. She was searching, but she didn't know what she was looking for. The back of Evan's church seemed as good a place to look as anywhere.

"The cross where Jesus was brutally nailed and died became a bridge for us. Until that time, the only way someone could truly see God was to live a perfect life. Guess what? No one qualified. Not one. So God became one of us, lived that perfect life, then suffered our punishment for us."

Carrie had heard this before. But what did he mean by the cross becoming a bridge?

"We cannot experience God on our own terms. No matter what you chant, no matter what else you might believe, God is unattainable your way. Jesus knew that. So He told His followers just before

He was led away to die, 'I am the way to the Father.' So we follow Him, and where does He lead us? Back to our Creator—the very personal God who loves us and wants us back!

"If we are to keep going, we must deal with the cross."

Carrie leaned forward in her seat, not wanting to miss one word.

"The cross becomes a bridge for us to walk across, leaving our own attempts to experience God and, when we reach the other side, taking hold of the hand of the One who was nailed to the cross.

"But," and here he stretched out his hands toward the audience, pleadingly, "you have to walk across the bridge.

"I'm telling you, none of us can make our own bridge. We all know it's true that we can't live a perfect life—we've tried and failed. And we might even like to dream up our own unique ways to get across the gap—to get to know God. But as Romans 3:23 says, we all fall short. Doesn't matter how close our custom-made bridge might get, if it can't reach, it can't reach.

"We have to come to Him on His terms. Jesus makes it crystal clear in John 14:6: 'I am the way and the truth and the life. No one comes to the Father except through me.' So here are your choices: You can come to God through the cross, or you can remain on your own tiny island. It's up to you. But in the end, there are simply no other options if you really want to find God.

"So how do you take the step? First, you have to agree with God that there is a gap between you and Him—we call it sin. Second, you have to agree that the bridge—Jesus' death on the cross and His resurrection—is there and that it's for you. And then you have to take the step across by giving your life to Him. It's that simple.

"That's what it's all about—joining with the Creator, as He intended you to do. That's why you were made. And I'm telling you from personal experience, it's the reason you exist."

Jim spoke for another few minutes, but Carrie was no longer

listening. When the service concluded with a song and a short prayer, Carrie left quickly and waited by the car. She kept quiet during the ride back to campus; she didn't want to talk to Evan— not yet. She had a lot to think about.

Or, rather, she *didn't* have much to think about. Just one thing. The cross as a bridge. A bridge from—how did Jim put it?—her own tiny island to this God she had been trying so hard to avoid.

Now, back in her dorm room, she looked at the circle before her. Words that had excited her just days before came flooding through her mind. *The sacred feminine.* Hieros Gamos. *Mary Magdalene. The Holy Grail.* She pushed these thoughts aside as she looked around the room for—ah! There it was.

She uncapped the black felt marker and walked over to the poster board. Starting at the upper-left corner of the paper, she drew an arching line that touched the top of the circle and continued to the upper-right corner. The arc was bigger than her circle. She stepped back and looked at what she had done.

God was real after all—the God of the Bible. She knew there must be a Supreme Person—not some force, but a Person who made her a person. That was the God she had been running from, and yet somehow running toward all this time—God, who made both male and female in all their uniqueness; God, who was far beyond the symbols humans made to represent Him. This God, who knew Carrie could not leave her tiny island by herself, had provided a bridge of escape. Because this God had for her what she would hope and expect from any other person … love.

God loved her, and He was waiting for her to cross.

Once again she picked up the marker. This time, she drew a cross, with the center point of the two lines right on top of the intersecting point of the arc and the circle. She thought about how *The Da Vinci Code*—the book that had caused her to examine the reality

239

of God in recent days—ends. She recalled that Robert Langdon, having made his way back to Paris, kneels before the spot where he believes Mary Magdalene's bones are buried.

Carrie, in the quietness of her room, also knelt down. But she was not kneeling before a dead woman. She was kneeling before the One who is alive. Carrie let go of her doubts; she let go of the wrong she had done; she let go of the pain she had experienced—and she knew she was accepted and forgiven and restored.

And that was when she could hear it almost audibly—Someone saying to her, "Welcome home."

For God so loved the world that he gave his one and only Son, that whoever believes in him shall not perish but have eternal life. John 3:16

Afterword

There are many more topics we would like to discuss with you related to *The Da Vinci Code*, but we do not have time or pages to do so in this book. **Is** there a question you were hoping we would answer but did not get to? **Help** is available. **For** those wishing to continue this study, you can visit one of the web sites listed below and explore to your heart's and mind's content.

The Da Vinci Code introduced a lot of questions about God, but offered many wrong answers. **Widows** and orphans (both literal and spiritual) are not well-served by speculation and wild tales, but by the truth about the One who declared Himself to be the way, the truth, and the life. "My beloved Son," God called Him in front of eyewitnesses. "Son of God," He called Himself. "Son of God," declared His apostles during and after His earthly life.

And **Son** of God, we believe, He truly is.

www.breakingthedavincicode.com
www.jimgarlow.com
www.cwipp.org

READERS' GUIDE TO
CRACKING DA VINCI'S CODE

You have read *The Da Vinci Code* and were left with many questions. Now you have read *Cracking Da Vinci's Code* and may have more questions. Don't let that alarm you. When on a quest for truth, questions are powerful tools. Do, however, be careful. Be careful to ask questions that increase discernment, not that feed skepticism. In other words, "be as shrewd as snakes and as innocent as doves" (Matthew 10:16).

The following questions are designed to help you work through any doubt or confusion you may be experiencing. Perhaps you will want to consider these by yourself or in a small group of friends; the key is to continue probing until you have found clarity. Keep in mind that even after much discussion you may not have all the answers, but you will have grown. God promises that "if you call out for insight … and search for it as for hidden treasure, then you will understand the fear of the LORD and find the knowledge of God" (Proverbs 2:3–5). And ultimately you will discover that there is but one Answer to all of the questions you will ever encounter. That Answer supersedes any code you will ever encounter. It is our desire that, if you do not already know the Answer, you will meet Him through what we have shared with you.

Blessings to you on your journey.

Chapter 1: The Code That Shook The World

1. How firm is your knowledge of who Jesus is? If your faith was challenged, could you defend it? How would you do it?

2. Do you think *The Da Vinci Code* poses a threat to Christianity? Why or why not?

3. *The Da Vinci Code* starts off with a declaration from the author that "all descriptions of artwork, architecture, documents, and secret rituals in this novel are accurate" [DVC, 1]. Do you believe that claim? How do you hope to benefit from studying *Cracking Da Vinci's Code*?

4. Brown wants you to "learn a ton" from his book. Do you think fiction is a good teaching device? Why or why not?

5. Pilate, when confronted with Jesus, asked the eternal question: "What is truth?" Is it possible to know absolute truth? Is there even such a thing as absolute truth or is truth relative to each person and each situation?

Chapter 2: God's Second Best Idea

1. Carrie Williams, the fictional character who begins each of our chapters from here out, experiences two "sexual shocks" in one day—the come-on by her boyfriend and finding out her room-mate is a lesbian. Do you think this is a fair representation of our culture today?

2. Do you agree with our statement that *"The Da Vinci Code* is ultimately—when pressed to its not-so-logical conclusion—an appeal for free sex, separate from the parameters established by God"? Why or why not?

3. Explain the differences between *agape* and *eros* love. How can you develop *agape* in your love for another person?

4. Do you see the Bible as a book that promotes "maximum sex"? Can you think of any passages other than those mentioned in our text that support this?

5. If sex is God's "second best" idea, what is His best idea?

Chapter 3: Women Are More Sacred and Feminine Than the "Sacred Feminine"

1. Looking at what the Bible has to say about women and at the history of women in the foundation of the church, how convincing is *The Da Vinci Code* in its claim that the church is a great oppressor of women? Do any of our arguments in this chapter satisfactorily counter that claim, as far as you are concerned? Why or why not?

2. In his very clever book of fiction, Brown makes up various facts to further his agenda. To give one example, he grossly exaggerates how many men and women were put to death during the Great Hunt era of the Middle Ages. (Contemporary research shows that there may have been 50–60,000 killed in comparison to Brown's five million.) Do you think *The Da Vinci Code* strives for accuracy or for emotional impact? Should the convictions we hold stem from one's intellect or one's heart? How do you balance the two?

3. We would not be fair if we did not acknowledge that some early church leaders did wrongly oppress women, even using the Bible to support their actions. Can one legitimately separate the actions of an individual from the organization he or she represents? Are there contemporary examples that come to mind? How do you determine responsibility?

4. Does *The Da Vinci Code* ultimately call for a celebration of the uniqueness of male and female or a blending of the two into one androgynous gender? How does the Bible differ from that? How do you respond to the premise that men and women are different?

Chapter 4: Jesus—Who Was He, Really?

1. Brown claims that Jesus was not considered divine until Constantine's time. We listed but a few of the early church leaders who wrote of Christ's divinity before the Council of Nicaea. How do you respond to Brown's assumption that Jesus was not divine? Do Jesus' human traits prove He wasn't divine? Why or why not?

2. Why was it important for Jesus to ask His friends who they thought He was? How would their answer change the way they thought about Jesus?

3. How is Paul, and the dates he wrote his letters, important to understanding the divinity of Jesus?

4. Is it important to you whether or not Jesus is truly divine? Why or why not? Who do *you* say Jesus is?

Chapter 5: Who Is Revising History?

1. Evan gives Carrie a lesson in the flying habits of geese. Just how does a flock of geese compare with how the church is supposed to function? Did you find the analogy helpful?

2. If history truly is just a "fable agreed upon," who are we to believe? How can we tell what version of history is the "truest"? Is there such a thing as true history?

3. Christian history seems to have many "losers"—those who committed great sins or who were killed for their faith. Yet *The Da Vinci Code* claims that church leaders—the winners—rewrote history to favor their "side." How do you respond to Brown's argument that winners write the history?

4. If you were a Christian when Constantine proclaimed religious tolerance and forced pagans to convert, how would you have

reacted to these new "Christians"? How do you think they would have reacted to you and your teachings? Would you have compromised your beliefs to "meet them in the middle?"

Chapter 6: Don't Shoot the Canon

1. If we did not have the Bible to follow, if we did as Marcion suggested and got rid of all scripture, what foundation would we have for moral law? What would keep each of us from doing what felt good at the time, regardless of the consequences to others?

2. Why is it important to know how our current Bible was assembled? Does this affect your personal faith?

3. Can a follower of Jesus dismiss the Old Testament as outdated and observe the New Testament only? Explain.

4. Our conviction that the Bible is the Word of God is based on faith *and* years of careful study. Do you believe that the Bible is trustworthy? Why or why not? Does that reasoning apply to the canon selection too?

5. After reading this chapter, do you believe that Constantine manipulated the formation of the canon? Or do you believe the canon was well established before the Council of Nicaea? Explain your stance.

Chapter 7: The Gnostic Gospels vs. the New Testament Gospels

1. Winston Churchill is credited with saying, "A lie gets halfway around the world before the truth has a chance to get its pants on." There are scholars, preachers, and authors—in this case, the fictional Professor Gibson—who repeat phrases that have been shown to be false, but by saying them often enough, such thoughts are nevertheless given credibility. How can we be open-minded while maintaining a strong sense of discernment?

2. Now that the Nag Hammadi texts have been "taken to the masses" through *The Da Vinci Code*, many people could begin to doubt the veracity of the Bible. If you hold the Bible to be the irrefutable Word of God, how will you defend it against these "secret scrolls?" If you do not base your beliefs on the Bible, do you trust the Nag Hammadi texts? Explain your choice.

3. Do you agree with the 1997 Gathering of Presbyterian Women that the four biblical Gospels are biased toward males? Should there be a Bible just for women?

4. If you follow the teaching of Gnosticism to its logical end, who will be your god?

5. We write, "Here we begin to decipher *The Da Vinci Code* and to suggest the real reason for its enormous popularity. The book appeals to many people because it expresses in such an engrossing way the new liberating religious option that has recently taken the West by storm." Where have you seen signs of this new religious option in our culture?

Chapter 8: Secret Knowledge

1. In the description of the *Hieros Gamos* rite, we learn that it is through this rite that men open their minds to receive knowledge from the divine. How does this pagan ritual treat the female partner?

2. What is the difference between "spirituality" and Christianity?

3. Contrast the pagan mantra ("You are at your best when you are not thinking") to the admonition in scripture to "take captive every thought to make it obedient to Christ" (2 Corinthians 10:5).

4. How do you define sin? Where does the concept of sin come from—man or God? What does the feeling of guilt have to do

with sin? Is sin a problem that needs to be dealt with or simply a part of life?

Chapter 9: The Clash of the Symbols

1. What roles do symbols play in the church? Do symbols play a part in your spiritual life?

2. What symbols are mentioned in the Bible? Which ones have positive connotations? Which ones have negative meanings?

3. Is it necessary to believe in a literal Satan in order to be a Christian? What would Satan's purpose be? Do you believe in Satan? Why or why not?

4. Why do you think some Christians are embracing the message of goddess worship?

Chapter 10: Cracking the Code

1. What does the phrase "The End of Days" mean to Christians? What does it mean to pagans?

2. What would a "non-Christian Jesus" look and act like? Does the world need a "non-Christian Jesus"?

3. The Goddess promises unity and peace. Does Christianity hold the same promise for everyone on earth?

4. What is meant by C. S. Lewis's comment, "God is a particular Thing"?

5. After reading *The Da Vinci Code*, was your image of Jesus changed? If so, how? Has your image of Jesus changed now that you have read *Cracking Da Vinci's Code*? How?

Notes

Chapter 1

1. Dan Brown, *The Da Vinci Code* (New York: Doubleday, 2003), 235.
2. David Klinghoffer, "Books, Arts and Manners," *National Review* (8 December 2003).
3. Dan Brown, interview by Matt Lauer, *The Today Show*, NBC, 9 June 2003.
4. *Bookpage* (April 2003).
5. Juli Cragg Hilliard, "ABC Special Examines Da Vinci Code Ideas," *Publishers Weekly*, Religion Bookline.

Chapter 2

1. C. S. Lewis, *The Four Loves* (New York: Harcourt, 1960).
2. Lynn Picknett and Clive Prince, *The Templar Revelation: Secret Guardians of the True Identity of Christ* (New York: Simon & Schuster, 1997), 158.
3. Lisa McLaughlin, *Time* (11 September 2000).

Chapter 3

1. Steven Goldberg, *Why Men Rule: a Theory of Male Dominance* (Chicago: Open Court, 1993), 14, 18, 35.
2. Alvin J. Schmidt, *Under the Influence* (Grand Rapids, MI: Zondervan, 2001), 98.
3. Verena Zinserling, *Women in Greece and Rome* (New York: Abner Schram, 1972), 39.
4. Jenny Gibbons, *Recent Developments in the study of the Great European Witch Hunt,* Covenant of the Goddess, http://www.cog.org/witch_hunt.html.
5. Ibid.
6. Ibid.
7. Ibid.
8. Ibid.
9. Robin Briggs, *Witches and Neighbors* (New York: Penguin, 1998).
10. Ross Clifford and Philip Johnson, *Jesus and the Gods of the New Age* (Victor Books: Colorado Springs, 2003).
11. http://www.cog.org/witch_hunt.html.
12. David Bercot, ed. *A Dictionary of Early Christian Beliefs* (Peabody, MA: Hendrickson), 692, 2 .419, 420.
13. Ibid., 693, 5.401.
14. Robin Morgan, *Women's Voices: Quotations by Women*, Jone Johnson Lewis, http://www.womenshistory.about.com/library/qu/blqumorg.htm.

Chapter 4

1. So well established are Paul's dates that few modern scholars, in their work on Paul, even bother to mention the subject. For instance an academic dissertation, directed by one of the most radical New Testament scholars of the modern era, Hendrikus Boers of Emory University, merely states in passing that Paul's argument in 1 Thessalonians is "fully in line with other examples of inter-Jewish polemic in the forties of the first century A.D." (see George Lyons, *Pauline Autobiography: Towards a New Understanding* [Atlanta, GA: Scholars Press, 1985], 203). The New Testament scholar, Elaine Pagels, whom we shall mention below, simply assumes without discussion the first-century dating of Paul, in order to write a book on the conflicting views of Paul, present in the church "as early as the second century" (see Elaine Pagels, *The Gnostic Paul* [Philadelphia: Fortress Press, 1975], 9).
2. Hans Conzelmann, *1 Corinthians: A Commentary on the first Epistle to the Corinthians—Hermeneia* (Philadelphia: Fortress Press, 1975), 251–254.
3. David Bercot, ed., *A Dictionary of Early Christian Beliefs* (Peabody, MA: Hendrickson, 1998), 93–100.

Chapter 5

1. http://priory-of-sion.com/psp/id22.html.
2. Michael Baigent, Richard Leigh, and Henry Lincoln, *Holy Blood, Holy Grail* (New York: Dell, 2004), 400.
3. Arthur F. J. Remy, *The Catholic Encyclopedia*, vol. VI, K. Knight. http://www.newadvent.org/cathen/06719a.htm.
4. Dan Brown, *Angels and Demons* (New York: Simon and Schuster, 2000), 110.

Chapter 6

1. Tertullian, *Against Marcion: The Anti-Nicene Fathers*, Alexander Roberts and James Donaldson, eds. (Grand Rapids, MI: Eerdmans, 1973), 272.
2. Irenaeus, *Against Heresies* 3:3:4.
3. Hermann Ridderbos, *The Authority of the New Testament Scriptures* (Philadelphia: Presbyterian and Reformed Publishing Company, 1963), 43.
4. Or something like that. It was actually Peter

Jones, *The Apostle Paul: A Second Moses to the New Covenant Community According to 2 Corinthians 2:14–4:6* (Princeton, NJ: Princeton Theological Seminary, 1973).

5. W. C. van Unnik, *The Jung Codex* (London, 1955), 125.

6. Ibid.

7. Graham Stanton, *Gospel Truth: New Light on Jesus and the Gospels* (Valley Forge, PA: Trinity Press International, 1995).

8. Carsten Peter Thiede, *The Earliest Gospel Manuscript?* (London, UK: Paternoster Press, 1992).

9. Martin Hengel, in 1985, in his "Titles of the Gospels," *Studies in the Gospel of Mark* (Minneapolis: Fortress Press), 64–84.

10. Hengel, ibid., gives the following reasons: "1. It is unlikely that the Gospels circulated without titles, if only for the purpose of introducing them; 2. the larger communities got hold of the Gospels quickly and needed titles to distinguish them; 3. if they circulated anonymously, how would a large variation of titles not arisen—but there is no MS evidence of this; 4. there is no evidence that some central authority in the second century existed which would have imposed a uniform nomenclature; 5. the imposition of the four Gospels was a slow process, where certain regions lagged behind others (in Rome there was hesitation over the Fourth Gospel); the regionality and far-flung nature of the second century church would suggest that the titles were established early on; 6. It is questionable that the first Gospel, of Mark, circulated anonymously [since it was not written by a well-known apostle]. Recipients from other communities would have wanted to know whether it came from a reliable source, and so it was no doubt sent, from the start, with the superscription—'the Gospel according to Mark.'"

11. Kurt Aland, *The Problem of the New Testament Canon* (London: Mowbray, 1962), 24.

12. Ibid., 18.

13. Phil Brennan, "Gibson: *Passion* Sprung from Suicide Thoughts," NewsMax.com (17 February 2004).

Chapter 7

1. See Elaine Pagels, *The Gnostic Gospels* (New York: Random House, 1971).

2. See James Robinson, *The Nag Hammadi Library in English* (New York: Harper and Row, 1977).

3. Bertil Gärtner, *The Theology of the Gospel According to Thomas* (New York: Harper &

Brothers, 1961), 11.

4. See John A. T. Robinson, *Redating the New Testament* (Philadelphia: Westminster John Knox, 1976).

5. See Colossians 2:16–19; 1 Timothy 4:1; Acts 20:29–30; 2 Peter 2:1; 1 John 2:18–19.

6. Duncan Greenlees, *The Gospel of the Gnostics* (Madras, India: The Theosophical Publishing House, 1958), vii.

7. Pagels, *The Gnostic Gospels*, 63.

8. *Thunder, Perfect Mind* 13:16-21.

9. See Elaine Pagels, *Beyond Belief: The Secret Gospel of Thomas* (New York: Random House, 2003).

Chapter 8

1. Gospel of Philip 70:5–10, cp. Gospel of Thomas 37.

2. Irenaeus, *Against Heresies* 1:21:3.

3. Epiphanius, ibid., 24.3:2.

4. Peter Jones, *The Gnostic Empire Strikes Back: An Old Heresy for the New Age* (Philipsburg, NJ: P&R, 1992).

5. George Trevelyan, *A Vision of the Aquarian Age* (Walpole, NH: Stillpoint Publishing, 1984), 161, cited in Ray Yungen, *A Time of Departing: How a Universal Spirituality Is Changing the Face of Christianity* (Silverton, OR: Light House Trails, 2002), 24. This is a useful introduction to the New Spirituality. The definitive work to date is by James A. Herrick, *The Making of the New Spirituality: The Eclipse of the Western Religious Tradition* (Downers Grove, IL: InterVarsity Press, 2003).

6. William Johnson, *Letters to Contemplatives* (New York: Orbis Books, 1991), cited in Yungen, ibid., 29.

7. See Stanislav Grof, *Future of Psychology: Lessons from Modern Consciousness Research* (New York: State University of New York Press, 2000), 5, for a list of time-honored techniques.

8. Stephen Prothero, *American Jesus: How the Son of God Became a National Icon* (New York: Farrar, Straus and Giroux, 2004), reviewed by Justin Pope, Associated Press (12 February 2004).

9. Leonardo da Vinci, *Leonardo on Art and the Artist* (Mineola, NY: Dover, 2002), 68.

9. "From the New Physics to Hinduism," karma2grace.org, http://www.karma2grace.org/articles.htm.

10. Barry Long, *Meditation: A Foundation Course* (Mullumbimby, AUS: Barry Long Books, 1996), 13.

11. *Tripartite Tractate* 124.21ff.

12. *Apocryphon of James* 4:19–21. Walter Burkert,

Ancient Mystery Cults (Cambridge, MA: Harvard University Press, 1987), 69, notes the very same tendency in pagan mystery religions.

13. My colleague in Old Testament assures me this is dime-store philology, but ingenious all the same.

14. See the apology for this claim in Virginia Ramey Mollenkott, Omnigender: A Trans-Religious Approach (Cleveland, OH: The Pilgrim Press, 2001), 41, 74.

15. Giovanni Filoramo A History of Gnosticism (Oxford, UK ; Cambridge, MA: B. Blackwell, 1990), 141.

16. Shirley MacLaine, Going Within: A Guide for Inner Transformation (New York: Bantam Books, 1989), 197.

17. Gospel of Truth 25:1–7.

18. Helen Shucman, A Course in Miracles (New York: Foundation for Inner Peace, 1975), 47, 262.

19. Lynn Vincent, "Underestimating Evil?" World (11 March 2000), 29. For more on this subject, see Peter Jones, Capturing the Pagan Mind (Nashville: Broadman and Holman, 2003), 75.

20. Hans-Martin Schenke (New Testament Apocrypha, vol. 1, 182–183) places it the second half of the second century (A.D. 150–200) because it shows signs of being written by the great Gnostic teacher, Valentinus, who was in Rome until A.D.165.

21. Wesley W. Isenberg, translator of the Gospel of Philip (see Robinson, The Nag Hammadi Library in English, 141), argues that since the Gospel of Philip contains clearly developed Valentinian teachings, it comes from an era after the life of Valentinus.

22. Burkert, Ancient Mystery Cults, 69.

Chapter 9

1. See historian of western secret societies David Livingston, The Dying God: The Hidden History of Western Civilization (New York: Writers Club Press, 2002), 2.

2. John Van Auken, Ancient Egyptian Mysticism and Its Relevance Today (Virginia Beach, VA: A.R.E. Press, 1999), 5.

3. "Circles," paragraphs 5–6. See Eugene Narrett, "Proud Ephemerals: Signs of Self-Made Men," Culture Wars (December 1999), 5.

4. Lynne Hume, Ancestral Power: The Dreaming Consciousness and Aboriginal Australians (Melbourne: Melbourne University Press, 2002), 79, 81.

5. Ross Clifford and Philip Johnson, Jesus and the Gods of the New Age (Victor Books: Colorado Springs, 2003), 54.

6. Grace Gedeon, "Sacred Circle as a Psychospiritual Practice and Its Role in Creating Conscious Community," GlobalRenaissanceAlliance.com.

7. Ibid.

8. Ibid.

9. The words of Dennis Kucinich, Democratic candidate in 2004, cited in World (25 October 2003), 14.

10. Altreligion.about.com.

11. Ravenonline.com.

12. Fabricia's Boschetto.com.

13. Skepdic.com.

14. To our knowledge, the only time the circle has been used in orthodox Christianity is to describe the unity of God, outside of the created circle.

15. Controverscial.com.

16. TheMystica.com.

17. TemplarHistory.com.

18. LuckyMojo.com.

19. Ibid.

20. ChurchofSatan.com.

21. Helen A. Berger, Evan A. Leach, and Leigh S. Shaffer, Voices from the Pagan Census: A National Survey of Witches and Neo-Pagans in the United States (Columbia, SC: University of South Carolina Press, 2003), 21–23.

22. Elaine Pagels, The Origin of Satan (New York: Random House, 1995).

23. Deena Metzger, cited in George Otis, The Twilight Labyrinth (Grand Rapids, MI: Baker Books, 1997), 107.

24. For the myth, see Robert Turcan, The Cults of the Roman Empire (Oxford, UK: Blackwell, 1996), 78–79.

25. Mark S. Smith, The Ugaritic Baal Cycle, Volume 1: Introduction with Text, Translation and Commentary of KTU 1.1–1. 2 (Leiden: New York: Köln: E. J. Brill, 1994), 102,105: "Anat's destruction of death . . . enables Baal's reappearance."

26. Martti Nissinen, Homoeroticism in the Biblical World: A Historical Perspective (Minneapolis: Fortress Press, 1998), 28.

27. Neal H. Walls, The Goddess Anat in Ugaritic Myth: SBL Dissertation Series 135 (Atlanta: Scholars Press, 1992), 83.

28. See Lucian, De Syria Dea, 50–51.

29. Richard Grigg, When God Becomes Goddess: The Transformation of American Religion (New York: Continuum, 1995), 22.

30. "The Return of Paganism: As Christianity Declines, Superstitions Gain Force," Zenit.org

(7 February 2004).

31. Jean Houston, *The Passion of Isis and Osiris: A Gateway to Transcendent Love* (New York: Ballantine, 1995), 2.

32. Hippolytus (A.D.170-263), in his *Refutation of All Heresies* 5:9:10.

33. Elinor Gadon, *The Once and Future Goddess: A Symbol for Our Time* (New York: Harper and Row, 1989).

34. Miriam Starhawk, "What Would the Goddess Do?" Belief Net, http://www.beliefnet.com/story/88/story_88 54_/.html.

35. Ibid., *The Power of Myth*, 58.

36. C. S. Lewis, *Miracles* (New York: MacMillan, 1947), 85, says: "The pantheist is led to state that either everything is God or that nothing is God, but in neither case is he able to give any precise meaning to his concept."

37. C. J. Bleeker, "Isis and Hathor," in Carl Olsen, ed., *The Book of the Goddess, Past and Present* (Long Grove, IL:Waveland Press, 2002), 32. The wisdom of Isis is recognized when the Egyptians call her "great in magic power."

38. Ibid., 38.

39. Burkert, *Ancient Mystery Cults*, 108.

40. Ibid.,112.

41. Ibid., 104.

42. Ibid., 97.

43. Burkert, *Ancient Mystery Cults*, 101.

44. See chapter 4, *Cracking Da Vinci's Code.*

45. Miriam Starhawk, *The Spiritual Dance: A Rebirth of the Ancient Religion of the Great Goddess* (New York: HarperCollins, 1979).

46. Wendy Hunter Roberts, *Celebrating Her: Feminist Ritualizing Comes of Age* (Cleveland, OH: The Pilgrim Press, 1998), see the Summer/Spring Catalog, 1999, The Pilgrim Press, the United Church of Christ publishing arm.

47. Sue Monk Kidd, *The Dance of the Dissident Daughter: A Woman's Journey from Christian Tradition to the Sacred Feminine* (San Francisco: Harper, 1996).

48. Amy Peck, "Our Mission," Center of the Sacred Feminine, http://www.sacred-feminine.org/page2.htm.

49. Mary Daly, *Beyond God the Father: Towards a Philosophy of Women's Liberation* (Boston: Beacon Press, 1973), 96.

Chapter 10

1. Bob Dylan, "The Times They Are A-Changin'," © 1963; renewed 1991 by Special Rider Music.

2. Riane Eisler, *The Chalice and the Blade: Our History, Our Future* (San Francisco: Harper and Row, 1987), 190, 194, 200. Eisler may be one of Brown's sources for this imagery.

3. Robin Lane Fox, *Pagans and Christians* (San Francisco: Harper & Row, 1986), 34. I have slightly modified the translation for the sake of clarity. This syncretism was already the case in Athens in the first century (see Acts 17).

4. Robert Turcan, *The Cults of the Roman Empire*, Antonia Nevill, trans. (Oxford, UK: Blackwell, 1996), 280.

5. Caitlín Matthews, *Sophia, Goddess of Wisdom: The Divine Feminine from Black Goddess to World Soul* (London: The Aquarian Press/Harper Collins, 1992), 330.

6. Diana L. Eck, *A New Religious America: How a "Christian Country" Has Become the World's Most Religiously Diverse Nation* (San Francisco: Harper, 2001), 77. Others have a similar goal. The Indian Hindu philosopher, Radhakrishnan, believes the "supreme task of our [present] generation … is to give a soul to our growing world consciousness," cited in ibid., 380.

7. The author of this book, Stephen Prothero, is a professor at Boston University.

8. Moshe Idel and Bernard McGinn, eds., *Mystical Union in Judaism, Christianity and Islam: An Ecumenical Dialogue* (New York: Continuum, 1996), 10–12.

9. Lewis, *Miracles*, 87. By this, Lewis means that God is not "universal being," that is, everything, because God has His own specific, determinate character.

10. Ibid., 90–91.

11. Cited in Adolf von Harnack, *Marcion: The Gospel of the Alien God*, John E. Steely and Lyle D. Bierma, trans. (Durham, NC: The Labyrinth Press, 1990), 72.

12. Ibid., 95.

13. Ibid., 96.

14. Greenlees, *The Gospel of the Gnostics* , vii.

15. See Peter Jones, *Capturing the Pagan Mind*, chapters 1–4.

16. There is perhaps one reference, on pages 95–96, though God here is ambiguously confused with Nature.

17. David L. Miller, *The New Polytheism: Rebirth of the Gods and Goddesses* (New York: Harper and Row, 1974), 4.

18. Bob Dylan, "Gotta Serve Somebody," © 1979 by Special Rider Music.

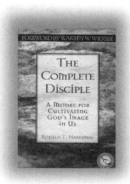

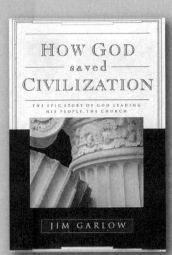
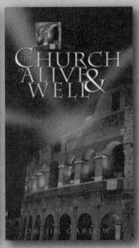
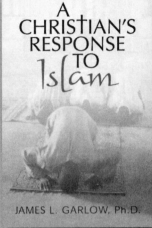

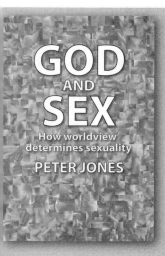

The Word at Work Around the World

A vital part of Cook Communications Ministries is our international outreach, Cook Communications Ministries International (CCMI). Your purchase of this book, and of other books and Christian-growth products from Cook, enables CCMI to provide Bibles and Christian literature to people in more than 150 languages in 65 countries.

Cook Communications Ministries is a not-for-profit, self-supporting organization. Revenues from sales of our books, Bible curricula, and other church and home products not only fund our U.S. ministry, but also fund our CCMI ministry around the world. One hundred percent of donations to CCMI go to our international literature programs.

CCMI reaches out internationally in three ways:

· Our premier International Christian Publishing Institute (ICPI) trains leaders from nationally led publishing houses around the world.

· We provide literature for pastors, evangelists, and Christian workers in their national language.

· We reach people at risk—refugees, AIDS victims, street children, and famine victims—with God's Word.

Word Power, God's Power

Faith Kidz, RiverOak, Honor, Life Journey, Victor, NexGen — every time you purchase a book produced by Cook Communications Ministries, you not only meet a vital personal need in your life or in the life of someone you love, but you're also a part of ministering to José in Colombia, Humberto in Chile, Gousa in India, or Lidiane in Brazil. You help make it possible for a pastor in China, a child in Peru, or a mother in West Africa to enjoy a life-changing book. And because you helped, children and adults around the world are learning God's Word and walking in his ways.

Thank you for your partnership in helping to disciple the world. May God bless you with the power of his Word in your life.

For more information about our
international ministries, visit www.ccmi.org.